IN PRAISE OF *MARKET LIKE YOU MEAN IT*

"This book is full of marketing treasures. Points are illustrated through entertaining examples and case studies of little-known and well-known marketing and media phenomena. Turbo charge your marketing with what you learn from this book."

—JOHN JANTSCH, AUTHOR OF *DUCT TAPE MARKETING* AND *DUCT TAPE SELLING*

"Grab this one! By investing in this book, you will discover how to cut through the marketing clutter to get noticed, be remembered, and get people talking, sharing, liking, tweeting, and buying."

—JOE VITALE, AUTHOR OF *HYPNOTIC WRITING* AND *BUYING TRANCES*

"Al Lautenslager is all business. He shows you how you need to step up your game to market like the pros. Buy *Market Like You Mean It* before your competition does."

—JEFFREY HAYZLETT, PRIMETIME TV SHOW HOST, BESTSELLING AUTHOR, AND SOMETIMES COWBOY

"The beauty of *Market Like You Mean It* is the wealth of practical information from somebody who has been there and done that. Al Lautenslager's advice is priceless. I strongly recommend this book."

—JOSEPH SUGARMAN, CHAIRMAN OF BLUBLOCKER CORPORATION

"*Market Like You Mean It* is chock-full of marketing treasures. Al Lautenslager illustrates his insights through entertaining examples and case studies of marketing and media phenomena. You'll accelerate your marketing with the fuel you'll find in this book."

—C.J. HAYDEN, AUTHOR OF *GET CLIENTS NOW!*

"Al Lautenslager presents an entertaining look at achieving total customer engagement and reveals how any-sized business can win long-term customers in today's overcrowded, highly distracted marketplace."

—MARC OSTROFSKY, *NEW YORK TIMES* BESTSELLING AUTHOR OF *GET RICH CLICK!* AND *WORD OF MOUSE*

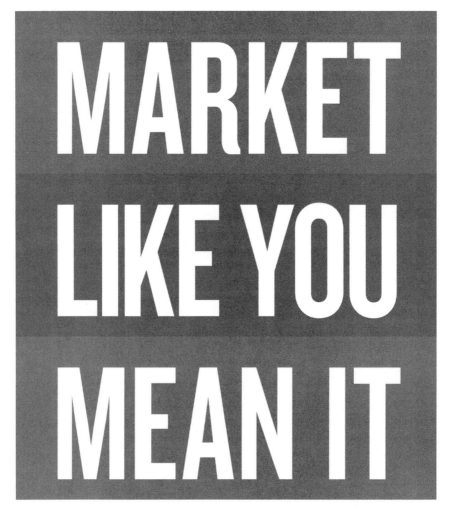

MARKET LIKE YOU MEAN IT

ENGAGE CUSTOMERS,
CREATE BRAND BELIEVERS,
AND GAIN FANS
FOR EVERYTHING YOU SELL

Entrepreneur
PRESS®

AL LAUTENSLAGER

Entrepreneur Press, Publisher
Cover Design: Andrew Welyczko
Production and Composition: Eliot House Productions

This publication is designed to provide accurate and authoritative information
in regard to the subject matter covered. It is sold with the understanding that the
publisher is not engaged in rendering legal, accounting or other professional services.
If legal advice or other expert assistance is required, the services of a competent
professional person should be sought.

Library of Congress Cataloging-in-Publication Data
Lautenslager, Al.
    Market like you mean it: engage customers, create brand believers, and gain fans
for everything you sell/by AlLautenslager.
    p.   cm.
    ISBN-13: 978-1-59918-535-4 (paperback)
    ISBN-10: 1-59918-535-0 (paperback)
    1. Marketing. 2. Internet marketing. I. Title.
    HF5415.L325 2014
    658.8—dc23   2014010830

Printed in the United States of America

18 17 16 15 14   10 9 8 7 6 5 4 3 2 1

Dedication

Someone once asked me, "What was one of the best gifts you have received?" My reply was that many times I get the opportunity to help entrepreneurs, business owners, and professionals of all types with their marketing and general business performance. I get the opportunity to see these same people succeed, reach new levels, and become prosperous as a result of my work with them. To me, that is a "gift" I get to receive. I dedicate this book to those and future professionals who will succeed and prosper in much the same way, as a result of this book.

CONTENTS

Acknowledgments xi

PREFACE

Getting Noticed, Remembered, and Talked About xiii

Part I

GET NOTICED

CHAPTER 1

Breaking Through Marketing Clutter .3
Messages Coming at You Now 4
Cutting Through the Clutter 5
The Mind at Work: The Psychology of Marketing 8
Busting Through the Content Marketing Deluge 10
Making a Commodity Business Stand Out 13
"AIDA" 15

CHAPTER 2

How to Survive the Marketing Message Storm 19
The Magic of Being Interesting 20

Excitement!. 21

Make a Dramatic/Compelling Statement 23

The Right Words for the Right Attention 25

Headlines! Get Your Headlines! 27

Billboard Marketing 32

Curiosity: Scott's Nametag. 34

Advertising Attention-Getters: Super Bowl Commercials 35

Political Ads 38

Engage with Emotional Needs. 39

The "Prankvertising" Trend in Marketing 41

The Repetition Factor of Marketing. 43

CHAPTER 3

It's All About the Story **47**

Stories Get Noticed and Remembered. 47

"TOMA": Top-of-Mind Awareness 50

CHAPTER 4

Wild, Wacky, and Bold: Using Humor to Get Noticed **59**

Kmart: Ship My Pants. 62

Church Signs 65

Veterinary Signs. 67

Funny Bar Signs. 67

Sometimes You Just Have to Ask to Get Noticed 68

Outrageous Gets Noticed. 69

Flash Mobs Get Noticed. 71

Men in Kilts 73

Red Bull Extreme Skydiver: Felix Baumgartner 74

Shocking 77

Surprise Marketing 80

Controversy 84

CHAPTER 5

The WOW Factor **89**

Luxury Gets Noticed. 90

Three-Dimensional Mail 91

Cute Puppies. 93

Mom-to-Be: Red Robin 95

CHAPTER 6

Getting Noticed Online **97**
Content 98
Getting Emails Noticed and Opened 99
The Marketing Hook. 102
Getting Noticed in Social Media Communities 103
How to Make Your Content Marketing Stand Out 107

Part II

GET REMEMBERED

CHAPTER 7

Motivating Customers and Prospects to Take Action **113**

CHAPTER 8

Social Psychology **117**
The Psychology Behind Social Transmission 117

CHAPTER 9

Mud on the Wall That Sticks: from
Attention to Engagement **123**
Taglines 125

CHAPTER 10

Your Mind at Work: The Power of Memory **129**
"Call Me Maybe"—Carly Rae Jepsen 131

CHAPTER 11

Taking Advantage of Competition **133**

CHAPTER 12

Guerrilla Marketing **137**

Part III

GET TALKED ABOUT

CHAPTER 13

Influence Marketing. **143**

CHAPTER 14

Buzz Happens **145**

Justin Bieber Gets Noticed 145

Beats™ by Dr. Dre™ 148

Relevance 150

Word-of-Mouth Matters 152

CHAPTER 15

It Takes a ~~Village~~ Community **155**

CHAPTER 16

Why Videos Go Viral **159**

WestJet 160

A Catchphrase Is Born: "Ain't Nobody Got Time for That" 161

Viral Thoughts 163

CHAPTER 17

Telling Friends **167**

Guinness Wheelchair Basketball 167

Four Seasons Heating and Air Conditioning:

Your Wife Is Hot 169

Sharing Osiris Shoes Customer Service with Friends 170

CHAPTER 18

Give Them Something to Talk About **173**

Buying Beer for 2,500 Will Get You Talked About 174

Using Bacon to Get Talked About: Bacon Buzz 174

Epilogue **177**

About the Author **181**

Other Books by Al Lautenslager 182

Index **183**

ACKNOWLEDGMENTS

THIS IS THE PART OF THE BOOK WHERE I GET TO OPEN MY HEART and express my gratitude, thanks, and love to those that support me, help me, love me, and help me keep the creative fires burning, now or in the past.

First and foremost, as in any acknowledgment for all that I have been given and all that I give, I acknowledge my awesome daughter Allison. I am so very proud of her no matter what and love her with all my heart. She inspires me daily even though our communication is less than that. She has turned out to be quite the young lady and is on her way to great things.

Secondly, there is the love of my life, best friend, and wife, Julie Ann. She supports me, cheers me, pushes me, and most of all, loves me. Life is at a whole new level with her. I hope everyone can eventually join me on cloud nine, where I now reside with her and because of her. Thanks for your support, Julie Ann, and I love you.

As in previous editions of my writing, I want to acknowledge my parents. I still quote my mother often, whether it is some of her entrepreneurial teachings, her superstitions, or her visions of great things that inspired me then and inspire me to this day. My dad, who is with her in heaven, had the great ability to tell it like it is and to interject his great sense of humor and warmth. Whether it was coaching, cheering, or his admiration of family, he was always there and his spirit continues to be present exactly at the right times. Thanks, Mom and Dad.

Family is always supportive and they help make it fun. In addition to those mentioned above, there are Bradley Gessler and Courtney Gessler-Brown; the rest of the ABCs of priorities for Julie Ann and I (Allison, Bradley, and Courtney). There is Max Simpson, a literary mentor, a scotch-drinking mentor, and the best father-in-law ever.

Acknowledgments wouldn't be complete without a thank-you of support for sisters, brothers, and in-laws (and cat Ivy). Thanks to my brother Steve Lautenslager and sisters Pam Gatliff and Karen Davenport and to in-laws Diane Prigmore and husband Marc and brother-in-law Steve Simpson. Whether you know when you are supporting or not, you are. For that, I thank all of you.

There are so many friends, professional acquaintances, and others that I would like to name but I am limited on pages here. To any and all who have touched me along my path, here is one big thank you.

There are more that will continue to join the circle. I am grateful for all of you and look forward to thanking you all again in future creations.

And then there's Lu.

GETTING NOTICED, REMEMBERED, AND TALKED ABOUT

CONSIDER THESE FACTS: MORE INFORMATION HAS BEEN PRO-duced in the last 20 years than in the previous 2,000. More than one million new websites are created every day. Marketing messages and their contribution to marketing noise are everywhere: banner-pulling biplanes over festival crowds and stadiums, rented advertising space on pregnant women's bellies, on urinal drain screens, on the side of bases at major league baseball games, and even now on most YouTube video postings. You know what happens on a visit to Times Square in New York City, and now smaller cities have similar massive light shows. So how is a marketer supposed to stand out and communicate? How can you connect and be heard by your target market?

I owned a successful business in a suburb of Chicago for more than 15 years. I continue to operate my own entrepreneurial ventures. To be successful in business today, I have found you must possess two things: One is a compelling and relevant product or service and the other is the ability to let those that can buy from you know about you. You can't have one without the other and be successful. The best product or service in the world that's also the best-kept secret is a pathway to failure. Letting people know about a marginal product or an inferior service is like spreading bad news; no one goes looking for it, they're not interested in it, and they'll soon seek out a better option.

Success is not built on copying something that is preferred. Success is not built on imitation. Being unique, standing out, and getting noticed are so much more important today than in times of yesterday. Twenty years ago, traditional, mainstream media was the primary marketing way to get the word out. Marketing messages could be turned on or off with the flick of a switch on the TV or radio, or open or closed in print ads.

Fast-forward to today's changing world of technology. Whether it's the World Wide Web, email, or ever-growing social media communities, commercial messages are now everywhere. Jay Walker-Smith of the Yankelovich consumer research firm reports that we've gone from being exposed to about 500 ads a day back in the 1970s to as many as 5,000 marketing messages a day today.

What, then, is the result of this marketing tsunami? Consumers and prospects (meaning people who don't know your product/service or haven't tried it yet, as opposed to existing or repeat customers) have learned to pick and choose what messages they pay attention to. Whether it's offline, in print, online, or on social media, marketers are faced with the task of becoming more creative, persistent, and sometimes crafty in order to get their messages heard; to get noticed. What hasn't changed in the online world is the need to get attention for your product or service. What has changed are the methods and platforms with which to do this.

Getting noticed is not a new challenge for marketers. The idea is simply a matter of communicating your message in an attention-getting way—whether it's in a headline, an email subject line, the first paragraph of a blog post, or the first few words in some traditional marketing vehicle like radio or TV.

It's not only getting noticed, though. That's just the first step. Imagine the most creative billboard in the world. Business is hard to transact upon viewing that billboard, so the message better be remembered, then acted upon after driving by. You have to get noticed, then remembered. That's what I did as a business owner. That contributed to my success. Getting remembered is the whole basis of the marketing concept of positioning. What do you want customers and prospects to remember about you? Taglines, for example, can position a business. Taglines can help you to remember a brand.

Without looking at logos, think about the taglines "Just Do It" or "Like a Rock." The mainstream public nearly always remembers Nike and Chevrolet, respectively, from those two taglines. Now think about Geico's common tagline, "15 minutes could save you 15% or more on car insurance." That's likely to be remembered, too. Geico, Nike, and Chevrolet, along with many others, have marketing messaging that works; each is remembered. These messages keep these brands at the top of mind of prospects so when and if they want the brand's related products or services, these brand "lights" tend to come on in their brains. That's the power of being remembered. Did they get noticed first? Of course they did, because although they certainly weren't the first in their categories to market themselves, they did it very effectively. Maybe it was Michael Jordan, shown jumping into the air on his Nike "Air" products, or a green gecko, or a frustrated caveman, but these brands first made you take notice and now they're talked about and remembered.

Red Bull took this to a new level. Their tagline, "Red Bull Gives You Wings," was the foundation of their sponsorship of extreme skydiver Felix Baumgartner. Baumgartner broke the sound barrier in a 24-mile space jump that shattered the existing record for the highest-altitude skydive. This is just one real example showcased in this book that any marketer can learn from.

Some call this marketing outrageously. In his book *Marketing Outrageously*, Jon Spoelstra says that outrageous marketing is the opposite of "professional" marketing; it may get you laughed at, and it might be politically incorrect, but it may also truly be the only safe way to spend money on marketing. We're really talking about breakthroughs here, not mediocrity. Getting noticed can lead to buying; getting remembered can lead to a transaction or action taken by a prospect, but getting talked about can be the ticket to a marketing eruption.

PART

I

GET
NOTICED

BREAKING THROUGH MARKETING CLUTTER

JUST LOOK AROUND. LOOK AT ALL THE MARKETING COMING your way. Marketing is all around you. As you're reading this, there are likely signs, radio commercials, point-of-purchase displays, labels, offers in your mail, TV ads, magazines lying around, salespeople, online advertising, social media, and on and on and on—all around you. Add all these up and the number of marketing messages you're exposed to every day usually amounts to more than 3,000; some say 5,000, and still others claim even more. Regardless, the point is that we are inundated by messages all day, every day. Walk into a grocery store or any retail establishment and this number soars. The same goes for the online content world; messages show up as blog posts, feature articles, special reports, slide presentations, infographics, downloads, webinars, online video, white papers, and more. The whole world of content marketing has exploded. Even if people do happen to set eyes on these messages, whether they actually take any notice is a different matter.

MESSAGES COMING AT YOU NOW

Messages that connect with your interests, needs, wants, and desires will lead you to stop, look, and listen to them, to take notice. The right message delivered in the right way to the right target gets noticed. If your target doesn't want or need what you are talking about, getting noticed will be a proverbial pipe dream. Messages coming at you that make you more aware of these wants and needs will also get noticed. Let's say that you have a dream home in your sights and you hear of ways to buy it and live in it; in this case, it's very likely that you'll take notice of these messages. Information about rental apartments, in this case, will not catch your attention.

Just think of a recent trip to the grocery store. Supermarkets are filled with a high density of messages, all of them screaming, "Buy me!" You don't notice every one of these messages while food shopping; you scan and look for the food items that fit your preferences. Sometimes you see new things and may explore further, but taking initial notice is related to something you like, need, or want.

Part of getting noticed involves reaching for the emotions of people that marketing messages are intended for. To get people to pay attention to your marketing messages, you need to find their emotions. Messages with no emotional connection are not noticed and certainly not acted upon. If you can make people feel happy, proud, nostalgic, or comforted, they will be far more likely to notice your message. When crafting your message, think about how it will hit those senses and feelings. Once your senses and emotions are stimulated, you will take notice and become interested in pursuing more information. That is the purpose of a headline, a starburst, or a graphic: to pull an interested reader or prospect into the next sequence of messaging.

Marketers are trained to put their messages where their target markets are or where they look. Looking and noticing are two different things.

Think about these differences. Think about satisfying needs, wants, and interests and you will get noticed.

CUTTING THROUGH THE CLUTTER

How does a marketer stand out in the crowded marketing storm? How can you, as a marketer, hit your target market right between the eyes? How can you cut through the media clutter that's all around you? Answering these questions represents the holy grail of marketing. In this section we'll talk about a few ways to break through the clutter; more ideas will be developed later in this book.

Every day there are new messaging ideas and repurposed content from thought leaders and marketers of all sizes and types, utilizing new methods that eventually come at you. If your messages are part of that clutter, your goal is to lift them above the clutter and get noticed. This book is full of ideas, stories, and situations that offer solutions to breaking through marketing clutter. Here are eight essentials to consider as you start off and move closer to that marketing holy grail:

1. *Focus on solutions.* This is what customers are really looking for. And when there is demand, half of your marketing job is done. Products and services that have a high demand get noticed early and often. Give your target market what they want or what they're interested in looking at. Offer something that shouts, "I'm a problem solver" or "I'm a solution" quickly and your message will get noticed.

2. *Aim at your target market.* Marketing that doesn't hit its intended target is classified as a waste, inefficient, or junk (as in "junk mail"). Marketing that does hit its target market is classified as interesting, effective, and very efficient. The key point here is to give your target market something that interests them. If you're a senior citizen interested in classical music, a direct-mail piece about the newest music releases for the latest rock-and-roll bands just won't do the job; you have no interest in that information. You're not part of the rock-and-roll music target market.

3. *Use headlines and subtitles.* Make these titles (and subtitles) provocative, thought-provoking, extreme, and completely unexpected.

Chapter 1 / Breaking Through Marketing Clutter

One of the best headlines I've seen—one I know got noticed—was, "Things the Government Won't Tell You About Terrorism." Another one that garnered equal attention, was "7 Mistakes Banks Make Every Day." Both would get my attention and make me want to read more.

4. *Have a crystal-clear message.* Graphics can get attention, but don't let them overwhelm your marketing to the point where your message isn't being communicated. The famous advertising guru David Ogilvy once said, "I do not regard advertising as an entertainment or an art form but as a medium of information. When I write an advertisement, I don't want you to tell me that you find it creative. I want you to find it so interesting that you buy the product." You can't bore people into taking notice with boring or unclear messages.

5. *Try extreme marketing messaging.* The truth is, extreme marketing works. Things that state the opposite, the negative, and mistakes get attention. Here are examples of headlines or messages that get noticed because of their extreme nature:

   – How to Run Your Company into the Ground in One Week
   – How to Make Your Salespeople 10 Percent More Efficient
   – How I Grew Profits by 0.005 Percent

   All these headlines would probably get your attention and make you want to read on because of their extreme nature.

6. *Offer a marketing hook.* This is another way to get noticed and it's especially prevalent in content marketing circles today. Simply put, information is offered as an incentive for additional contact. This "hooks" a prospect into the fold, setting the stage for further communication. That's what I did as a business owner. One of my hooks was offering a list of "99 Direct Marketing Tips." Another hook that I offered on my website was a special report titled "50 People to Instantly Add to Your Network." People wanted that information. Offering the information separated me from the competition and customers and prospects became hooked. Here are other examples of hooks: .

   – Call us today for a free mortgage loan calculator.

– Download a free recipe ebook using our spices and seasonings.

– Stop by today for a free vase for your Mother's Day flowers.

All these hooks offer something of value to an interested prospect. They'll all increase not only the attention your pieces get but your response rates as well.

If you're using print marketing to communicate to your target market, put these hooks in a starburst graphic. If it's in an audio or video format, make it extreme, loud, and memorable. Online browsers and shoppers respond to free downloads and interesting and relevant content, including ebooks, top-ten lists, checklists, guides, workbooks, and more.

7. *Leverage odd items, shapes, and sizes.* Another thing to consider when you want your pieces to stand out from the crowd is to create something that's a different size or has a different tone or is otherwise outside the normal format. This includes odd-shaped mailing pieces, extreme colors or messages, and choosing unusual times at which to approach your target market, like talking about Christmas in the spring. Carlsbad Brewery once dropped fake passports in the New York City subway system to notify their target market about a new product they were launching. Finding a passport on the subway was unexpected; it's not something you see every day. Carlsbad's messages got noticed.

8. *Answer directly "What's in it for the prospect?"* Holiday Inn Express advertised that their motels had the "number-one customer-rated showerhead." Have you ever been asked to rate a showerhead? Holiday Inn discovered this was important to their target market and communicated that message directly to them. You can listen and read all about the features of a Holiday Inn Express, but hearing about the number-one customer-rated showerhead speaks to something *all* visitors want. What's in it for them? A superior shower. Superior showers get noticed.

Standing out from the marketing clutter will always be a marketer's challenge. Starting with these fundamentals will help you break through.

THE MIND AT WORK: THE PSYCHOLOGY OF MARKETING

Much has been written about the role of psychology in marketing. Understanding how the human mind works as it relates to marketing is fundamental to getting noticed. Marketers work every day at understanding how customers act, think, and feel—all toward the ultimate goal of getting prospects and customers to buy. *The Oxford American Dictionary* defines *psychology* as the scientific study of the human mind and its functions, especially those affecting behavior in a given context. Marketing is an attempt to influence behavior.

Understanding acting, thinking, and feeling is the core of psychology. Psychologists study behavior surrounding these essential functions. Much of behavior as it relates to marketing centers around how people react to brands, products, services, benefits, wants, needs, and more.

Social media is at the forefront of marketing psychology. Consider the following: I learned, as a business owner, that people do business with people. They don't do business with a logo or a tagline. Sure, identity and image further relationships, but we all still ultimately conduct our business with one another. This is part of our inherent need to participate with others in the form of a community. That is the essence of social media: belonging to and engaging with and within a community. People also notice people. They might notice what is being said, appearances, and actions, but we all pay attention to the *person* who is speaking or acting, or who we're simply looking at. *Noticing* people or a person is the first step toward developing a relationship.

Relationships turn into sales. The number-one reason people buy from anyone is trust. People buy from people they like, people they know, and people they trust. Think about vendors or customers you speak to on a regular basis. When you drop your dry cleaning off at the cleaners, do you have a conversation at the counter with the same person every time? Do you feel that they know you and that you know them? Do you talk about the community, family, or other common interests? If not at the cleaners, you probably have your spots within your community where this happens. It may even be in an online community. These conversations, connections, and relationships build trust, which strengthens relationships. That is the foundation of buying and selling.

In psychology, trust is believing that the person who is trusted will do what is expected. From a psychological standpoint, trust is integral to the idea of social influence: It is easier to influence or persuade someone who is trusting and it's easier to be influenced or persuaded by someone who is trusted. Trust is a major factor that creates relationships between people.

Just look at trust at work when considering the opinion or recommendation of a close friend compared to hearing an advertisement on the radio or seeing one in print. The personal recommendation ranks significantly higher. People trust their friends; they don't always trust advertising. We are inclined to notice and buy from those we are in a relationship with and we value that more than many other factors.

People buy with their heart, not their head. You may be able to give me dozens of logical reasons why you would buy something, but if it is not felt first, it won't be noticed, and secondly, it won't be bought. It's true that some people approach buying decisions with more logic than others, but most make purchases based on their emotional state at the time—how they feel, not what is logical.

Customers and prospects choose products based on all kinds of factors. Usually, it's impossible to influence every factor, so a successful marketer needs to balance the factors of getting noticed, appealing to emotion, and catering to the rational decision-making process—all parts of personality.

Investopedia describes the "halo effect" as a marketing term to explain the positive bias shown by customers toward certain products because of a favorable experience with other products made by the same manufacturer. Put another way, if you like one food manufacturer's brand of soup, the halo effect makes it likelier you'll buy another flavor of the soup they make, and perhaps buy their other products as well. Investopedia goes on to state that, basically, the halo effect is driven by "brand equity," that is, one brand earning more money than another brand because consumers feel that a known brand name is worth more than a lesser-known brand name.

The halo effect suggests that you will buy from someone because you like them. Like them and they get noticed. Like them and you like their message. Like them and you usually like what they are selling. That's the power of a social relationship.

There is a psychological notion that says people will react to and especially notice the unconventional versus the conventional. Put another way, one marketing psychologist noted that the novel trumps the conventional every time. If someone walks into a rodeo wearing a pinstripe suit and sunglasses, he gets noticed. If he is in cowboy attire, chances are he will blend in and not be noticed; in that situation he would be conventional. Interesting gets noticed. Things do not have to be shocking, off-the-charts, obnoxious, or too extreme, but blending in typically does not get attention. That is the psychology that leads to buying. This leads to not only getting noticed but getting talked about.

As a final point here, I'm not asking all marketers to become psychologists. That's not necessary to successfully market a product. Understanding how purchase decisions are made and the balance between emotions, relationships, and rationality does go a long way, though. Achieving the right balance of these key factors will get you noticed in a cluttered world.

BUSTING THROUGH THE CONTENT MARKETING DELUGE

Unless you have been living under a rock, you know that most of the world has dramatically integrated social media marketing into daily life. Social media has been the proverbial game-changer in both our business and personal lives. This dynamic genre of marketing is always changing and is only becoming more and more powerful.

Word-of-mouth has always possessed that power. Social media has made that bigger, faster, and more immediate. People can now influence each other more than ever, creating what has been called the biggest revolution to hit marketing since TV.

Now putting social media and marketing influence into overdrive is the whole field of content marketing. Fundamentally, content marketing dispenses content of all kinds, to all takers, all the time. Content can take any number of forms: social media posts, blogs, websites, articles, slideshows, webinars, podcasts, white papers, video, photos, and more.

This staggering amount of content only adds to the barrage of marketing messages. With so much new and repurposed content, in so many forms, and new thought leaders in this field, it's becoming easier to get lost in the content storm. That's not a good thing if you are a passionate marketer. Getting content noticed is what you are passionate about. Paying attention to getting noticed is now as important as generating and repurposing the content itself.

This book is full of examples on getting noticed, getting remembered, and getting talked about. Many of these I have experienced or observed. These intentional forms of marketing represent "marketing like you mean it" at its fullest. Let's break content marketing down into a few parts and apply them directly to getting content that will stand out in the aforementioned tsunami.

CONTENT TOPICS

Coming up with compelling content topics is the lifeblood of content marketing. Ask yourself, "What ideas can I generate that are related to helping others do something, think of something, or have a new point of view? What ideas can I think of that will prevent mistakes, solve problems, or share successes?" The flow of engaging, relevant ideas will keep the content that informs your content marketing program in strong form. Repurposing some of these ideas will create even more ideas. Getting ideas from target market members, including customers' and prospects' "pain points," is always a great start to content generation.

All of the following ideas are content topics that come from reusing or reformatting one original article. That is the essence of repurposing content. Let's look at examples of the components involved in content repurposing, all generated from one original article called "Ten Ways to Improve Sales in the Coming Year:"

- ! *Blog post.* Take each of the ten ways in the article and create a blog post for each.
- ! *Twitter, LinkedIn, and Facebook.* Post links to each blog post on Twitter and Facebook.
- ! *SlideShare.* Create a slideshow called "A Step-by-Step Process to Increasing Your Sales This Year."
- ! *Webinar.* Using the slides from SlideShare and the content from the original article, develop and present a webinar: "Hot Sales Techniques You Can Implement Today."

! *Ebook.* "Preventing These Selling Mistakes Will Improve Your Sales."

! *PDF download.* "Sales Improvement Checklist."

TENDING TO PAIN POINTS

In marketing, solutions are what people pay for. In the world of content you should always be providing information that's helping to answer the question, "What's in it for me, the prospect?" This means not only supplying content that is solution-oriented but content that helps readers avoid the pain they are experiencing from a particular problem or challenge. The pain point is the burning need a customer or prospect has for something. They tend to be highly motivated to eliminate or alleviate this pain by accepting your solution. For example, imagine a bank offering a loan package that can be received with a signature on one page. This solves the pain point of signing so many documents at loan closing. Think about the restaurant that offers a guide on how to eat nutritiously and lose weight when eating out. This solves the pain point of restaurant food that is high in calories and fat. If there is a benefit to what you're offering, then it answers the question of what is in it for the prospect. Content needs to talk to all of these to stand out and get noticed.

RELEVANT, FRESH, AND INTERESTING CONTENT CREATES TRUST

You can't bore people into paying attention. That means you better have content that is interesting, relevant, and fresh; these characteristics are meaningful to both prospects and existing customers. Meaningful information is the engine that creates trust in companies, people, and brands—the connection that's so essential to all types of marketing, on- and offline. Trust can be built with testimonials or endorsements from a trusted influencer outside of a company. That trust makes targets welcome new marketing messages and fresh content, creating positive reactions and results over time.

ENGAGEMENT AND RELATIONSHIPS

Nothing gets noticed more than communication from a friend or someone that you know. In the world of marketing—whether content, social media, or any other kind—you are very often noticed by the relationships you establish and maintain. Relationships are opportunities for engagement. Engagement gets noticed and spreads content.

For example, a restaurant can establish relationships with customers in order to increase repeat visits from customers. These relationships also increase loyalty in the process. Some of my favorite restaurants make their website and blog a place for me to find menu items, nutrition articles, and dining tips. Like me, other visitors come back to the site to learn from the content and we feel more connected to the restaurant, that there is a true relationship and we are more likely to not only remember the restaurant but tell our friends about it and return for another dining experience.

CONTENT PACKAGING

Graphics—design, images, logos, branding, colors, and more—get noticed more than words. Graphics are an opportunity to package content in a form that's different, stands out, is interesting, and gets noticed. This includes the marketing vehicle that the content is contained in. Maybe your prospects prefer newsletters, blogs, websites, and maybe even an offline marketing vehicle. Pictures, titles, headlines, and subheadings are all part of the content packaging. Jetsetter, an online community of travelers that provides members with insider access, expert knowledge, and exclusive deals on the world's greatest vacations, uses a very simple photographic display of vacation destinations to get click-throughs and site conversions.

There are certainly more ideas than this for content marketing, but these are essential. They'll help you stay on the right marketing track and get you noticed amid the marketing tsunami that's hitting right now in the form of content marketing.

MAKING A COMMODITY BUSINESS STAND OUT

Sometimes businesses struggle with finding their unique selling proposition, what makes them different from all the other businesses in their category. Some struggle to find a unique point of positioning. At times, that differentiating factor is found by digging deep to really understand *why* customers buy from you and only you. Other times it is more deceiving. Many times, the brand is the same, the service offering is the same, and the products offered are identical, or nearly so. Differentiation, getting noticed, standing out is the challenge that exists in a marketing world where many things are the same. This is not an impossibility, though. Here are considerations for standing out in that congruent world.

EXPERT POSITIONING

The whole concept of positioning is creating a perception that stands out in a prospect or customer's mind. Giving others the perception of being an expert, i.e. expert positioning, makes you stand out in people's minds. People trust experts. People like to buy from experts. People have confidence in experts, whether companies that are experts or people who are experts. Companies and people that know what they are doing and convey skill and confidence differentiate themselves from competitors who have less expertise. I have no qualms stating that I am a marketing expert. Be sure that you can back up whatever expertise you profess.

MARKET KNOWLEDGE

Knowing current trends and sharing new ideas differentiates. Differentiation is required to stand out. Market knowledge also includes knowing competitive situations, offerings, solutions, advantages, and the like. Being able to talk with customers and prospects about this is advantageous and fuels that all-important relationship that leads to selling. Knowing the market also leads to offering just the right solutions for customers and prospects. That's the kind of thing prospects notice that makes them customers, and that customers notice to make them repeat customers.

RELATIONSHIP MARKETING

At the end of the day, the difference between your business and a competitor's business, if you can't find any other differences, is you. That is why many customers notice you and do business with you. Your business is the only one that has you. People may buy from you because of the relationship they have with you: They like you, they know you, and they trust you. They may go out of their way to keep that likability alive and well. That's the type of company/person you want to do business with. You can tell when a competitor doesn't try to get to know you or doesn't like you; in these cases, the trust never develops. Likability and relationships are definitely differentiators.

Is it possible to stand out? These factors prove that it is.

"AIDA"

No, this section is not about the four-act Italian opera by Giuseppe Verdi. This AIDA refers to an acronym often used in marketing that describes how consumers engage with marketing messages:

A **Attention**. Sometimes "awareness" is used for the A. It's about getting the customer's or prospect's attention.

I **Interest**. Oftentimes, interest is related to benefits and competitive advantages of products and services. Interest allows the prospect to continue on with the marketing message: If there's no interest, there's no attention.

D **Desire**. This refers to playing on emotions and psychology. In convincing prospects that they want and desire something, their interest will continue and lead to the last letter in this acronym.

A **Action**. This refers to motivating customers and prospects to take action as a result of the marketing messaging viewed.

According to Wikipedia, the AIDA term and approach are commonly attributed to American advertising and sales pioneer E. St. Elmo Lewis. In one of his publications on advertising and marketing, Lewis mentioned three principles to which an advertisement should conform:

The mission of an advertisement is to attract a reader, so that he will look at the advertisement and start to read it; then to interest him, so that he will continue to read it; then to convince him, so that when he has read it he will believe it. If an advertisement contains these three qualities of success, it is a successful advertisement.

Just a quick note: In this case "advertisement" is used instead of the more general term, used throughout this book, "marketing." The AIDA formula has been used in many ways over the past century. It is recognized as an important driving force in marketing messaging, copywriting for advertising and public relations (PR), speech-writing, commercial scripts, blog posts, and content development.

Attention is what this book is about. Attention is the initial reaction of getting noticed. It could be a headline, a graphic, or a provocative statement. All of this is to catch a reader's eye and make him stop, take notice, and continue reading your message. This point of contact and point of attention is generally at the beginning of a message or delivery. The result, ideally, is that the reader wants more; he wants to venture further into a message. Other forms of attention-getting include shocking or extreme statements; new information; and interesting story lines.

To get someone else's attention it's essential to stop thinking like a marketer and start thinking like those whose attention you're trying to attract. Get into their mind and influence their thinking. Part of your goal is to have your prospects feel a bond with your message and product and to respond to you favorably, supported by marketing messages.

Once attention is gained—once something gets *noticed*—moving a reader (and a prospective or existing customer) to the point of increased interest is the next marketing challenge. Interest is about engaging with prospects so that they want to spend their valuable time understanding your message more.

Many times, marketing messages are delivered in an interruptive fashion. First, they have to get noticed, but to engage the target of the message requires the building of interest. Talking the language of your prospect is a great start here. Can your prospects identify with what is being communicated? Speaking clearly and accurately builds interest. At no point do you want to confuse the prospect. This diminishes interest, for sure. Speak from the standpoint of your audience; what's in it for them? Answering this question well will help you increase interest.

Once an audience or prospect is interested in something, you want to feed that interest. This is a point in the marketing process where you can help them "feel" what you're communicating, and it may also be a way to eliminate a pain point and enhance desire. For example, your marketing message might state what life would be like without that pain point as another way to increase desire. Understanding customer/prospect emotions will help you to communicate with them in the right way.

Helping them to avoid pain, overcome fears, and feel joy and pride are just a few emotions that boost the desire factor. Lastly, anything related to a potential solution to the prospect's challenges will increase desire.

The whole purpose of marketing is to motivate prospects and customers to take action. That action, many times, is a purchase. It could also be a recommendation, a trial, or comparing one product or service to another. Understanding exactly what is motivating to your customer or potential customer is the final step of the AIDA formula.

Make sure you tell your readers and prospects what to do. In marketing this is the "call to action." Do not leave it to chance that a prospect knows what action to take as a result of the marketing messages; prospects need to be told what to do. The more specific the call to action, the better the response will be. All marketing messages should have a call to action associated with them. Some examples include:

! "Call us today!"
! Visit our website.
! Enter our contest.
! Contact us for more information.
! Stop by our place of business.
! Register for a free webinar.

In Chapter 2 let's explore some real, out-of-the-box methods for making sure your message gets heard above the whirlwind sweeping up your target audience's attention.

2

HOW TO SURVIVE THE MARKETING MESSAGE STORM

IT'S PRETTY OBVIOUS THAT NO ONE IS GOING TO TAKE NOTICE OF anything unless it's interesting.

Dos Equis beer knows this. The Most Interesting Man in the World is a character in an advertising campaign for Dos Equis that started airing in late 2006. The advertisements feature a bearded, debonair, elderly gentleman proclaiming a montage of daring exploits involving him, "the most interesting man in the world," and performed in his younger years. What makes his "Most Interesting Man" character interesting are moments that would lead anyone to take notice, such as: at museums, he's allowed to touch the art; his blood smells like cologne; sharks have a week dedicated to him; he once had an awkward moment, just to see how it feels; the police often question him, just because they find him interesting; he freed an angry bear from a trap; he once parallel-parked a train; and his two cents are worth $37 and change.

At the end of the advertisement, the man—usually shown sitting in a club or other social setting surrounded by several women—says, "I don't always drink beer, but when I do, I prefer Dos Equis." Each commercial ends with his signature sign-off: "Stay thirsty, my friends." This campaign *is* interesting. Interesting gets noticed and it works. The agency responsible for the creativity of this Dos Equis campaign describes the man as "a man rich in stories and experiences, much the way the audience hopes to be in the future."

THE MAGIC OF BEING INTERESTING

Was "interesting" effective? According to Dos Equis, U.S. sales increased each year after the ad campaign started and even tripled in one year shortly after the campaign started, all while imported beer sales were declining for other brands. Being interesting works.

While Dos Equis masters the art of being interesting with a dashing older gentleman, there are other ways to get noticed by being interesting. Try incorporating these into your next marketing brainstorming session:

! Be funny

! Be obnoxious (without crossing the line)

! Be controversial

! Surprise people

! Be an authority

! Predict the future

! Share discoveries and experiences

! Be unconventional

! Be weird

! Ignore the rules (but stay within the law)

! Introduce people to new things

! Foster your uniqueness

! Make the routine memorable

! Be curious

! Fascinate people

! Ask questions and challenge the norm

The opposite of being interesting is, of course, being boring. Marketing guru Seth Godin states that, "If the marketplace isn't talking about you, there's a reason. If people aren't discussing your products, your services, your cause, your movement, or your career, there's a reason. The reason is that you're boring."

Blogger Scott Ginsberg states that nobody notices normal. Nobody buys boring. And nobody pays for average. There are endless ways to be interesting, but sticking to these principles should get you noticed, remembered, and talked about.

MARKETING TRUTH

No one takes notice of anything unless it's interesting.

EXCITEMENT!

We all know that if something is exciting, it will get noticed. Most people not only take notice of something exciting, they react to it. If people are excited about products, services, or messages, they are naturally more likely to engage with the service or product and become a customer. Excitement is the opposite of boring and we've already stated you cannot bore people into a relationship or into buying.

Creating buzz is another way to describe the generating of excitement. Campaigns that are designed to stimulate others can do so with excitement. Buzz marketing and marketing with excitement is designed to "wow" those that receive messages.

"Buzz marketing" is a viral marketing technique that attempts to meet a consumer with a unique, spontaneous, and sometimes outrageous message instead of the usual calculated marketing pitch that sounds like it came from the standard formula used by an advertising agency. Unique, spontaneous, and outrageous are exciting after all, right? They will get noticed.

Apple is perhaps the master of buzz and excitement; they've been able to generate great interest in their products. People take notice when Apple wants them to take notice because of this "excitement" approach to marketing new and existing products. The excitement Apple generates makes customers camp out in line for days ahead of the release of a new product or a new generation of an existing product. Marketing your product before it's ready for release to customers creates the kind of excitement that gets Apple's products noticed and sold.

Excitement is something that arouses a strong response, but it's a marketing concept that's easier to talk about than execute. Here are a few methods to consider when building excitement that will get you noticed:

- ! *Create a brand voice that connects with your audience.* This may be a voice of authority, a voice with an attitude, or some type of "in your face" messaging.

- ! *Don't rely on the same old advertising scripts.* Dull, monotonous copy is boring. Make messages shorter, fun, and engaging.

- ! *Show your passion.* Bliss, obsession, and enthusiasm all foster excitement.

- ! *Deliver marketing messages to your target markets and prospects with a high level of energy.* People enjoy high energy and are more likely to notice your messages when delivered with a lot of enthusiasm and pep.

- ! *Communicate as if something is the best, most unique thing in the world.* You have heard phrases like "the best thing since sliced bread" or "the best thing since canned beer." Talk about what makes your product or service the best thing ever.

- ! *Show others that you're very happy to be talking to them.* Happiness is contagious and is a form of excitement.

- ! *It's exciting to be the sole expert of something.* When you are the go-to person, people are excited to meet you if you have something they want. Make your prospect feel that you are that go-to person. That's exciting!

Creating excitement is truly a mindset. People will see right through anything fake. Excitement is your gift to those that receive your marketing message. Think that, and you and they will both share in excitement. Communicate with energy and enthusiasm and even an exclamation along the way.

In marketing we talk about motivating prospects to take action. Someone once said that nothing gets done until someone gets excited. Excitement is a motivator. Take advantage of that when marketing. Show your passion. Get someone else excited so they take action. Enthusiasm is a contagious emotion.

Think yourself into this mindset: You are making a great improvement in someone's life. You are, in turn, passionate about your marketing. Make sure that energy and enthusiasm comes across in your tone of voice. That is the essence of truly marketing like you mean it.

Whether you're giving a speech, talking on the phone, or presenting one-on-one, your tone, your nonverbal actions, and your expressions all play an important role in showing excitement and enthusiasm to others.

MARKETING TRUTH

Excitement motivates people to take action.

MAKE A DRAMATIC/COMPELLING STATEMENT

As you look around, the storm of marketing messages continues; many times it seems never-ending and great marketers are always watching for opportunities to stand out in the storm. Making a dramatic or compelling statement is another storm survival technique. This is akin to creating an attention-getting headline. Dramatic statements in any part of a marketing message get attention:

"Things the Government Won't Tell You about Terrorism"
"Triple Your Income and Take More Time Off"
"Your Co-Worker Is about to Have a Heart Attack and You Can Prevent It"
"Four Things the FBI Can Do with Your Smartphone When It Is Powered Off"

Another attention-getting technique online or offline in marketing messaging is asking a provocative question. Webster defines provocative as "causing annoyance, anger, or another strong reaction, deliberately." Here are some examples:

> "Why Aren't You Making as Much Money as 95% of Your Graduating Class?"
>
> "Why Do You Pay More for Health Insurance Than All Your Neighbors?"
>
> "Is the Lottery Really the Best Retirement Plan?"
>
> "Are You Satisfied Living Paycheck to Paycheck?"

Provocative questions stimulate your prospects, compelling them to find out more about what you are offering.

Personalizing your statements or questions also makes them more compelling and dramatic, attracting attention quickly and effectively. When communicating one-on-one, using someone's name is the number-one attention getter. Take one of the provocative questions above and insert someone's name in it, and you get a double attention-getter. You can personalize messages with other personal information, but be careful of being perceived as a stalker. When personalizing questions or statements for a group, you can talk in terms of a common denominator for the group. For example, if you're talking to a group of college seniors about their job prospects after graduation you could say, "Remember your first day of college?" Or to a group of parents you might ask, "When you were growing up did your mom and dad always warn you against doing things you're now warning your children about?" Any time someone sees a statement or question and thinks, "Ah, that's me," you've got their attention.

MARKETING TRUTH

Dramatic and compelling statements are the headlines of your marketing.

THE RIGHT WORDS FOR THE RIGHT ATTENTION

When your prospects see your marketing messages they have three choices: They can completely ignore it. They can scan it. Or they can read every word offered to them. Getting your prospects to choose number three is the goal of marketing—and the goal of your messaging.

Your messaging is primarily made up of words, phrases, and sentences. The common denominator of these three is the words. Using the right words with the right impact gets attention over using the wrong words, which leads to scanning or completely skipping a message. We've already talked about the amount of marketing messaging that's constantly bombarding you every day. Add to this today's connected world and we truly do start to go numb or immune to the marketing noise. Some even call it online attention deficit syndrome. Attention spans, as a result, have gotten way shorter. Tweeting, Facebook, YouTube, and more have made us all lazy readers. Your goal as a marketer is to keep your marketing up with these changes in communication.

It takes the right words, phrases, and sentences to hit your target square between the eyes, which means you have to choose and use the right words and phrases. Some call these "power" words; others call them "impact" words and phrases; and some have referred to the right words as "action" words. Regardless of the name you use, it's the words that need crafting. These words typically get quick attention:

- ! Convenient
- ! Achieve
- ! Critical
- ! Easy
- ! Now
- ! Proven
- ! Fast

Let's take a look at this in action:

> *Before*: "Our investment guide is better than anything that has been published for the investor market. Try it and see."

After choosing new words: "Increase the value of your portfolio by 30% by year-end with our proven and easy-to-use methods."

Which would you buy? Which words got your attention? Notice the difference in the words in each. So many times marketers want to think all about themselves. Focusing on your prospect with a specific outcome is more effective, especially when the outcome is exactly what the target market is wanting.

It's not about what you have to offer or need to sell. It's always about what your prospective customer needs or wants to buy. That's what should determine your word choice, just like in the example above. That determines how much you'll get noticed.

Different marketers will try to succeed with different "impact" words, depending on the product or service marketed and the target. Based on my own survey work, this is a list of the more popular impact words (in no particular order):

Accomplish	Hot	Results
Achieve	How-to	Revolutionary
Benefit	Impact	Safe
Best	Improve	Save
Breakthrough	Instant	Secrets
Compelling	Learn	Simple
Convenient	Love	Solution
Critical	Money	Special
Discover	More	Step-by-step
Dependable	New	Unique
Easy	Now	Unlimited
Excellent	Peace of Mind	Ultimate
Exciting	Personalized	Unprecedented
Free	Promise	Yes
Fun	Proven	You
Guaranteed	Quality	Your
Healthy	Quick	

Really understand your target market. Think about what they react to. Find where they hang out online, read publications they read, understand what they pay attention to, and then check the words used in all these marketing vehicles. Those are the words that work with your target market. Use these in your offers, your headlines, your calls to action, and other marketing messaging. Also pay attention to changes in markets, customer demands, and marketing. Impact words will evolve over time. Until then you will do well with the list above.

Before we leave this section, let's look at one particular impact word: the use of the word YOU. The primary reasons we all act are because we believe our actions will benefit us, satisfy us, or make us feel better. If we hear that something is going to benefit us we will pay attention. If we understand that marketers are talking to us and only us, we will feel special. Here's an example of the use of the word "you" in a marketing message:

Before the use of the word "you": All users of social media marketing could benefit from a faster computer, a larger video screen, and a great speaker system if they tweet daily, if they watch lots of videos, and if they market online.

After the use of the word "you": As a user of social media marketing you could benefit from a faster computer, a larger video screen, and a great speaker system if you tweet daily, if you watch lots of videos, and if you market online.

It seems simple at first but read it again. You will see the difference and the impact.

MARKETING TRUTH

It takes the right words, phrases, and sentences to hit your target square between the eyes.

HEADLINES! GET YOUR HEADLINES!

Whether you read the newspaper, magazine, newsletter, or website, you scan. *What* do you scan? Pictures and headlines, mostly. What happens when you see a headline that you're interested in? You stop and read underneath the headline—the article that goes with that headline. Headlines feed your attention, whether online or in print.

You've not only heard it over and over, you've experienced it over and over. You know that the headline is often the most important part of any content you read. Why do you think that is? It's because it saves you time and prevents you from diving into the text of an article or paragraph that you're not really interested in. (That's assuming the headline is pertinent to the text, of course.) Is it safe to assume that all authors write great headlines to capture their readers' attention right away? No, of course not. Many headlines don't do the job that headlines are supposed to do.

You only have the briefest of moments to grab someone's attention during those scans. Some headlines are boring and simply don't pull a reader further into a story. You know the importance of that first impression you make on your reader. Without that attention-grabbing, "get noticed" headline, your first impression becomes no impression. Crafting a headline that is purposeful becomes the number-one job of the writer; a very critical element in written communication. The more compelling or attention-getting a headline is, the higher the probability of getting what you've written seen and read by a larger audience.

We've mentioned magazines, newspapers, and online content when discussing headlines. There is one more very important headline consideration, and that is in email communication. The headline in this case is the subject line of the email. Emails are very often opened based only on the scan of a subject line, especially in an overloaded email inbox. So crafting the subject line with the same attention-grabbing power as you would anything else in your marketing campaign is essential in email communication, too. Think headlines when crafting your subject line.

Another version of a compelling headline is in search engine results. When you do your respective search for your keyword or a phrase, the resulting links on the search engine results page are a collection of headlines. You scan and click on the one that interests you the most or comes closest to what you were thinking when you initiated your search.

Our mission here is to provide you the tools and information to get noticed. In order for you to get noticed you have to think from the standpoint of those you are targeting with your message or information. In marketing, you want to speak from the perspective of the customer or prospect. Every time they look at your marketing, they're thinking, "What's in it for me?" That means you have to grab them to make them read on. With every communication, think about what will cause them to read on. That's the start of how to craft a compelling headline. Spend time on this—*lots* of time. Don't release your communication until you're convinced you have a headline that will get noticed. Once you do, you will get more attention, more readers, more buzz, and more results.

One of my first lessons in understanding headlines was reading the issues of *National Enquirer* that my mother bought in the grocery store checkout lane. John Caples, a legend in advertising for more than 60 years, served as one of the most effective copywriters in the history of advertising. As a fledgling copywriter in 1926 he wrote one of the most famous advertising headlines ever: "They Laughed When I Sat Down at the Piano. But When I Started to Play!—" This headline was part of an ad that pointed out that you could teach yourself to be an accomplished musician and play virtually any musical instrument. Caples is also known for his 1931 book, *Tested Advertising Methods.* As an expert in direct-response advertising, Caples mastered results-oriented, direct-response mail-order copy. He was known for stressing simplicity and getting to the point quickly, the exact formula for a compelling headline.

Here is Caples' counsel to all crafters of marketing messages:

Advice to copywriters: When you are assigned to write an ad, write lots of headlines first. Spend hours writing headlines—or days if necessary. If you can come up with a good headline, you are almost sure to have a good ad. But even the greatest writer can't save an ad with a poor headline.

As long as we are citing marketing gurus, David Ogilvy, hailed as the father of advertising, stated that, "On the average, five times as many people read the headline than read the body copy. If you haven't done some selling in your headline, you've wasted 80 percent of your money. The wickedest of all sins is to run an advertisement without a headline."

By now you can see that if your headline doesn't get attention or get noticed and pull readers into the rest of your message, the rest of your marketing is meaningless.

Headlines are natural ways to get attention. They stand out visually so you almost have to pay attention to them first. Consider headlines a time-management tool. A headline that doesn't get your attention is a signal to you to keep on scanning other headlines until you find one worth reading more about. Also, headlines make for easier reading, which contributes to a higher comprehension level.

Create your headlines to get noticed, get attention, and to inspire interest. The more compelling and interesting your headline, the higher the probability of attracting the target you are after. And don't forget about subheadings. Let's look at some different kinds of headlines that worked.

How-To Headlines

In marketing, motivating people to take action is typically the goal. Reading a how-to headline usually leaves no doubt about what's next:

- ! Five Activities That Will Extend Your Life
- ! How to Double Your Income and Take More Time Off
- ! Paying Your House Off in Five Years

Story Headlines

In this book you will read more about the power of a story. While you can't tell a story with just a headline, you can introduce a storyline as a hook:

- ! How a Five-Year-Old Saved a Life
- ! From Ds and Fs to CEO
- ! Alive! How I Survived Burial in an Avalanche for 12 Hours

Challenge Headlines

If you can get a prospect or a reader to connect with what you wrote, you have a good chance of communicating further with them. If you pose a "challenge question" and a prospect says, "That's just like me or my situation," you've got their attention:

> ! Would You Like More Customers Than You Can Handle?
> ! Are You Faced with More Debt Than You Could Ever Pay Off?
> ! Is Your Teen Struggling to Get Through High School?

EXTREME HEADLINES

Sometimes referred to as "shock and awe" or "surprise" messaging, extreme approaches definitely get attention:

> ! One in 20 People Will Get Arrested This Year
> ! Seven Foods to Eat to Guarantee a Shorter Life
> ! What Your Car Dealer Won't Tell You

TARGETED HEADLINES

Over half of the success of your marketing is based on targeting. The wrong message may be sent to the right target and still get a response, but the right message sent to the wrong targets gets little or no response. So the more targeted you can make a headline, the higher the probability it will be read—especially by those you want to read it:

> ! You've Thought about Retiring But Don't Know Where to Start (target: people in their 40s to 60s)
> ! If You Want a Good College Education for Your Child, You'll Like This (target: parents of high school/college-age children)
> ! Want a New Job You Really Like? Read What *Not* to Do (target: people who are unhappy in their current job or want to advance in their career)

EMOTION-BASED HEADLINES

In every area of marketing, playing on emotion works, whether in a headline or in the body copy of marketing messages. Emotions drive us whether we think we are rational or not. Here are some examples:

> ! Someone You Know Is About to Have a Heart Attack—And You Can Prevent It
> ! Live Longer with Less Stress Over Money

！ Your Kids Will Struggle to Have the Same Quality of Life That You Do

Very often you only have a brief moment to get attention and get noticed. Headlines can do that for you efficiently and effectively.

MARKETING TRUTH

Without a compelling, attention-grabbing headline,
your first impression becomes no impression.

BILLBOARD MARKETING

Billboard marketing is designed to catch a prospect's attention fast. The goal is for the billboard to first get noticed, then get remembered. These are two distinct goals, because you want people to remember the billboard's marketing message once they've passed it. You only have a very short amount of time to make this happen, since billboards are usually read by people passing by at a high speed. To be effective, a few catchy words accompanied by attractive and compelling graphics are key. A billboard must get noticed immediately; the rule of thumb is that you have eight seconds to grab the driver's attention.

Even if you don't realize it, billboards are all around us, and you pass by many more than you think and many more than you remember. With all the marketing messages coming at a prospect, once again, standing out is key. While the short time to get noticed seems like a weakness, it can be a strength if the right target market sees the right message in the right way. As we've mentioned, this is the case with all marketing messages.

Here are ways to ensure that your billboard gets noticed:

！ *Use as few words as possible.* Think in terms of between four and seven words. If you only have eight seconds, this amount is about all you have time for. Drivers going by at a high speed want something easy to read, and fewer words are, of course, easier to read and process. If your message requires more words, it's probably better to find another marketing vehicle.

❗ *Use extreme headlines or in-your-face graphics.* This may border on being a distraction to drivers, but extreme billboards get noticed and talked about.

❗ *Don't ask prospects to do something.* Billboards can be effective for image advertising or building a brand and awareness. But asking your potential customers to take action with a billboard message is very often ineffective. Sometimes people will remember a compelling website or a phone number in a jingle, but don't consider your billboard a mechanism to elicit a direct response.

❗ *Be interesting.* We've said it here before: You can't bore people into buying something. You also can't bore them into taking notice of you. Clever is good, but don't make your target audience work too hard to figure something out on a billboard. Remember, you only have eight seconds.

❗ *Target what you're saying and where you're saying it.* Put your message where your target market is. Billboards can be especially effective if the market you're trying to reach is in a concentrated area and you know many will drive by your board.

Electronic billboards—which use animation and bright lights—are becoming more popular and are great ways to get attention.

Billboard marketing works best if there's a significant graphic component to the marketing message. The one component that is almost a slam dunk for billboard effectiveness and attention-getting is creativity. This could mean using the space outside of the billboard. Bic Razor "shaved" the grass in front of a blank billboard with a stand-up, life-size razor leaning against the billboard. The "shaved" grass got attention. A California Audi automobile dealer marketed their latest and greatest luxury car with a headline challenging rival BMW: "It's Your Move,

---

MARKETING TRUTH

The keys to effective billboard marketing are a few catchy words accompanied by compelling, visually attractive graphics.

Chapter 2 / How to Survive the Marketing Message Storm

BMW," the billboard said. BMW countered by erecting a billboard on the other side of the road featuring their latest and greatest luxury vehicle and the headline "Checkmate." It got noticed. Similarly, Ford Motor Company thought outside the billboard when they installed a smoke machine behind the billboard to pump in smoke to show a spinning rear wheel burn-out on a featured Ford car.

CURIOSITY: SCOTT'S NAMETAG

Scott Ginsberg really understands marketing and how to stick out from the crowd. So how does he do it? How does Scott Ginsberg get noticed? He wears a nametag everywhere he goes (he even has a tattoo of a nametag) and has done so since 2000. A YouTube video about Scott says that "he turns rare into remarkable." And remarkable gets noticed. People see his nametag wherever he is, and they take notice. Scott Ginsberg has turned this noticeability into a business of being a highly sought-after keynote speaker and an international sensation, all by being remarkable, sticking out, and getting noticed. Scott has built a business around the brand of Scott Ginsberg, the name-badge guy. I've met Scott. I've seen his nametag. I remember Scott because of this.

Scott's expertise is "approachability." He works with organizations of all types, helping their employees to become more approachable. Scott Ginsberg believes that wearing nametags make people more open and friendly, the foundation of his business. Scott is in the business of helping others increase not only their approachability but their marketability. He does something different—something wacky, yet convincing. Scott Ginsberg is in the business of getting noticed. Scott's websites get more than 30,000 hits every day from people all over the world. His blog ranks in the top 100 because he wears a nametag everywhere he goes. He succeeded because he separated himself from the rest of the keynote speakers and marketers in the marketplace.

Remarkable doesn't come easy. It's not something ordered off the shelf. Scott's lesson is to do something completely unique and opposite of the status quo. He is proof that doing so can lead to success. Scott Ginsberg understands how to get noticed. Take a look at the titles of some of his recent blog posts and look for the uniqueness in the topics he covers and his approach to these subjects:

- ❗ How to Build a Thought Leadership Platform so Clients Come to You with Money
- ❗ The Secret to Turning Browsers into Buyers
- ❗ Keys to Becoming More Approachable and More Referable in Business
- ❗ How to Make Yourself Memorable in Networking Conversations

I first took notice when I saw Scott and his nametag. That got my attention. That got noticed. What are you doing to get noticed?

MARKETING TRUTH

Do something completely unique and opposite of the status quo.

ADVERTISING ATTENTION-GETTERS: SUPER BOWL COMMERCIALS

The Super Bowl is a special American event shown every year to many millions of viewers worldwide. It is now even more special in the advertising world because it is most likely the only mass advertising opportunity left for the big brands. I review Super Bowl commercials for TV and radio stations and am interviewed on air the day after the Super Bowl to discuss my reviews. There is continual debate as to whether more product gets sold, business increases, or even that brands get noticed from their Super Bowl TV ads. Just like other marketing, getting noticed by your prospects or customers is the necessary first step. It used to be said that nothing happens until something is sold. Now it can be said that nothing happens until something gets noticed. One way Super Bowl advertiser and fashion retailer H&M got attention was to show soccer hunk David Beckham in his underwear when the company rolled out a new line of Beckham's bodywear. The North American marketing director for H&M stated that, "We've got everything we need to make this ad a success. We've got a global sports icon, the biggest stage in the world, and an amazing product."

Are these enough to get noticed? Even though the Super Bowl is the single most-watched TV event of the year, advertisers still have to work hard for advertisements to get noticed. Not only do ads have to get noticed on TV when shown, they are competing for eyeballs because of the many other distractions going on at the same time: bathroom breaks, trips to the kitchen, taunting from opposing team fans, nachos and beer. On top of all this people are double-screening: tweeting on their smartphones, viewing videos on their tablet devices, and more. Despite these limitations, every year there are commercials that get noticed and talked about. Here are a few ways to make both of those happen in your own marketing messages:

- ! *Nostalgia.* Many old TV shows, movies, and products never get *too* old.

- ! *Repetition.* Ninety percent of purchase decisions are made with the subconscious mind. The way to reach the subconscious is with repetition. That logic holds for Super Bowl commercials, too. Budweiser is the number-one advertiser during the Super Bowl and has been advertising during the game for years. Budweiser's approach to gaining attention is to reach a mass audience; if you want to get noticed, show up more.

- ! *Weirdness.* A recent Super Bowl commercial featured Bar Refaeli making out with Jesse Heiman, an unknown actor—until he was in the commercial.

- ! *Celebrity appearances.* Whether it's the Dos Equis Most Interesting Man in the World, Tiger Woods, or Oprah, stars almost always get noticed in an ad. Chances are you still remember Betty White in the Snickers Super Bowl ad.

- ! *Animals galore.* Not just the Budweiser Clydesdales, but also monkeys, dogs, cats, and more get noticed, usually in a humorous or cute way (it works).

- ! *Extreme actions.* This is another way to say "people doing stupid things." Simply put, obnoxious gets noticed, which probably says something about the demographics of people who watch the Super Bowl.

! *Sexy women.* This is almost a "duh," considering the number of men watching the big game. Think Cindy Crawford drinking a Pepsi or Ali Landry eating a Dorito, or almost every GoDaddy.com ad (aired or not). The biggest understatement in this book may be this: Sexy women get noticed.

Bob Parsons, CEO of infamous Super Bowl advertiser GoDaddy. com, stated that the intent of the first GoDaddy.com ad (one featuring a wardrobe malfunction) was to "attract the attention of 90 million viewers, many of which are engaged in conversation and well on their way to being at the legal limit of intoxication." Danica Patrick, the sexy race car driver and talent in many GoDaddy.com commercials, commented that, "The spirit of the commercials is to be edgy and fun and push the envelope a little bit, but also add a little bit of funny personality to them." Bob Parsons and Danica Patrick know what will get noticed in a Super Bowl commercial.

Getting noticed is one thing; selling products with a TV commercial is another. Bill McKendry, founder and chief creative officer of branding and marketing firm Hanon McKendry in Grand Rapids, Michigan, states that, "Sex and humor are great at getting people's attention . . . but the challenge is that they always take people's eye off the ball and they don't remember who the ad is for; they forget the brand."

Marketing guru Robert Kolt, of Kolt Communications, states "You want [the ads] to be memorable, you want to create some buzz, and you want people to know there is a product link . . . You can get almost too funny and wrapped up in a story that you forget to sell your product." You want to get noticed, but you also want to get remembered with a

---

MARKETING TRUTH

You want to get noticed, but you also want to get remembered—with a purpose.

Chapter 2 / How to Survive the Marketing Message Storm

purpose. Super Bowl commercials are not hobbies; each has a goal to hit after getting noticed.

Sexy models and outrageous skits attract eyeballs longer and get more media attention than commercials focused on customers using actual products.

POLITICAL ADS

Why do we see so much negative advertising around election time? The simple answer to this question is because it works. It works because negative political ads get noticed and get talked about. Getting talked about wins elections. In political campaigns, the goal is to rise above a cluttered media and advertising landscape. Sometimes there is total disregard to the outrageousness of a message. Who took notice of Hillary Clinton's campaign ad in the 2008 Democratic primaries, when the ad warned that opposing candidate Barack Obama was not ready to face a national security threat in the middle of the night? This came on the heels of Republican Senate candidate Carly Fiorina releasing the "demon sheep" ad showing video of red-eyed sheep and accusing her rival of being a wolf in sheep's clothing. Both of these ads got noticed and talked about throughout the campaign.

Chris LeHane, a Democratic political strategist, states "Negative campaign advertising is a knife fight in a telephone booth, and there is no conventional referee out there who is going to throw a flag that makes a difference, so there's no downside. These ads drive the larger media narrative of a campaign, and the stories and coverage of the ads and rhetoric will often have a bigger impact than the original ads or comments." Obviously, they get noticed.

MARKETING TRUTH

Media coverage of the ads and the ads' rhetoric will often have a bigger impact than the ads themselves.

We have spoken already about using emotion to get noticed. Negative campaign advertising plays very much on emotions to rise above the fray and noise; specifically, these messages play on feelings of fear and doubt. Add uncertainty and a crisis like a poor economy or a war and you have a winning formula for getting noticed in a negative way. This type of advertising gets supporters committed and excited.

ENGAGE WITH EMOTIONAL NEEDS

Whether it's the copy in an article, a headline, a blog post, a tweet, or an email, making an emotional connection with your reader will increase the probability of your content getting noticed. Without that all-essential emotional connection, you will get passed by, ignored, or people will stop reading.

Marketing is all about emotional connections. Effective marketing makes its target *feel* something, followed by *doing* something. The key to making both of these happen is to focus on the emotions of your target market. Most marketers work very hard at convincing their targets why they should buy their products and services. Marketing and selling is more than that. It's a matter of telling your target how they will feel better, smarter, avoid pain, look better, or even reach euphoria as their personal or professional goals are met.

The words you use to get attention, to make an emotional bond, and to create effective marketing are the keys to the necessary connection to get noticed and remembered. Let's look at some primary triggers that pivot on emotional connections:

! *Immediate gratification of desires.* Messages that have an element of instant gratification sell directly to those who want a product or service. The key here is focusing on the emotional link to that want. Your messages should build a sense of urgency that supports instant gratification, i.e., buy right now, this offer will expire soon; only three units left; and "download immediately."

! *Fear.* We all know that fear is a motivator. It's also a powerful emotion to feed on in order to get noticed, to get read and remembered, and to motivate people to take action. Can your headlines, bullet points, calls to action, or other messaging components induce fear? Fear is very popular in insurance sales and marketing. Fear is also induced by communicating what happens if a product or service is *not* bought. Go ahead and be bold here; hit your target right between the eyes with fear and you will get noticed.

! *Trust.* The number-one reason people buy your products and services is trust. Trust can be built with emotional connections. Good quality, good service, a great reputation, and effective communication all build trust with audiences. Trust is the thing that makes people buy a "want" even if there is not a true need. Nothing else works without trust.

The Harvard Business Review blog reported on specific emotions that were common to content that was shared virally online. These emotions included:

! Curiosity

! Amazement

! Interest

! Astonishment

! Uncertainty

Direct-marketing experts agree that the seven most powerful emotional hooks are greed, guilt, anger, flattery, fear, exclusivity, and salvation. Messages that include something related to one of these will get noticed, remembered, and talked about.

Other emotions to consider that trigger attention:

! Lust

! Vanity

! Pride

! Envy

! A desire to look good

! Comfort and pleasure

! A desire to be liked and loved

! Scarcity

! Less hassle

> ## MARKETING TRUTH
>
> *Marketing is all about emotional triggers.*

It's a fact that customers buy on emotions, not necessarily logic. Successful marketing will focus on the emotional triggers that feed the wants of a consumer. Getting noticed and remembered are triggered by the same emotions. Think about which emotion you will focus on before creating your headline, message, or content.

THE "PRANKVERTISING" TREND IN MARKETING

The 'sNice coffee shop was the setting for a shock-and-surprise promotional stunt for the movie remake of *Carrie*, a great example of a marketing trend known as "prankvertising." With marketers finding it increasingly challenging to effectively draw attention using traditional channels, other "virality-seeking," out-of-the-box techniques such as prankvertising are gaining traction. Prankvertising is outrageous or risky marketing stunts that include "pranking" unsuspecting people with a prank or spectacular stunt. Most are recorded and the hope is that the video footage will then go viral. Marketers, and especially advertising and marketing agencies, are always fighting to outdo each other with creative, attention-getting productions designed to shock and surprise.

As I said, the key component to using prankvertising as an advertising strategy is the tricking, scaring, or pranking of an unsuspecting person or audience. This is consistent with today's emphasis on content marketing; just think of it as a different type of content that's being delivered. Playing jokes on people to promote something has been around for many years; even prankvertising isn't new. It actually existed before the advent of digital marketing, but marketers are increasingly using this technique, taking full advantage of the virality-boosting tools available online. This not only saves on spending for expensive TV spot production and air time but generates free public relations (PR) and media coverage with plenty of buzz when something goes viral. Prankvertising events are effective if they are shared through social media, online mentions, and websites of participating marketers.

Although prankvertising marketing stunts are not new, brands and marketers are looking more to this tactic, taking the stunts to a sometimes extreme level and using increasingly sophisticated, spine-tingling, hair-raising, and occasionally horrifying scenarios to break through the clutter and complexity of the many marketing messages thrown at consumers.

Imagine that you're waiting for the elevator in a high-rise office building, minding your own business. The doors open and you're met by two men wrestling intensely on the floor, fists flying, bodies thrashing, in an obvious fight. One of the men wraps a cord around the neck of his adversary, pulls it as tight as he can, choking the life out of his opponent, literally. If you felt shock and surprise at witnessing this, that would probably be an understatement. You have just witnessed another example of prankvertising. In this case the two men were actors. The actors' stunt and your reaction to it was being filmed by a viral marketing agency as part of an extreme event to promote the movie *Dead Man Down*.

Prankvertising mimics the old days of the TV show *Candid Camera*, hosted by Allen Funt. Mr. Funt was about 50 years ahead of his time, taking unsuspecting victims into strange, ridiculous, funny, and sometimes embarrassing scenarios and situations, in full public view. The prankvertising difference is the magnitude of the prank. Prankvertising is *Candid Camera* or any of the hidden camera shows on TV today, on steroids, all with a sponsor's name attached. The *Dead Man Down* elevator prank is a very vivid example of this. "We engaged people by putting that strangulation [a plot point in the

---

MARKETING TRUTH

Content is a great way to keep your brand top of mind among your target market members, even if the content is "prankvertising." The more extreme these stunts are, the more buzz they typically generate.

movie] into a real-life setting" and challenging folks to examine their own reactions when coming upon such a scene, says James Percelay, founder of Thinkmodo, an agency known for staging wild marketing stunts. Prankvertising gets noticed, and the more extreme it is, the more people talk about it.

THE REPETITION FACTOR OF MARKETING

The last technique for surviving the "marketing message storm" is repetition. Up to 95 percent of our decisions are made by the subconscious mind. The way to enter into that subconscious mind is through repetition. Whether subconscious or conscious, the concept behind repetition is that when a potential customer wants or needs a particular product, your product will come to mind first; marketers call this "top-of-mind awareness." L.L. Bean, Victoria's Secret, and other reputable companies mail catalogs over and over, even when those receiving them don't make purchases. That's because they want you to remember their brand when you think of the products they sell. You may think, "Oh yeah, I keep getting their catalog." Or you may think, "I need a new pair of hunting boots, so I'll check L.L. Bean because they keep sending me a catalog." Others that think in the same way eventually buy. That sale is attributed to repetition. You take notice because your mind has been touched many times by the messaging from that brand, over and over and over.

It's often said that a prospect or your target market member needs to be "touched" six to eight times before they're in purchase-readiness mode. That means that they will think of you first when they want or need your product or service. A single ad in the newspaper won't do it. A single postcard in the mail won't do it. Prospects need to be touched many times, in many ways.

Thomas Smith, a London marketer, once wrote a guide called *Successful Advertising*. It was written in 1885. Here's what Mr. Smith wrote back then:

> The first time people look at any given ad, they don't even see it. The second time, they don't notice it. The third time, they are aware that it is there. The fourth time, they have a fleeting

sense that they've seen it somewhere before. The fifth time, they actually read the ad. The sixth time they thumb their nose at it. The seventh time, they start to get a little irritated with it. The eighth time, they start to think, here's that confounded ad again. The ninth time, they start to wonder if they're missing out on something. The tenth time, they ask their friends and neighbors if they've tried it. The eleventh time, they wonder how the company is paying for all these ads. The twelfth time, they start to think that it must be a good product. The thirteenth time, they start to feel the product has value. The fourteenth time, they start to remember wanting a product exactly like this for a long time. The fifteenth time, they start to yearn for it because they can't afford to buy it. The sixteenth time, they accept the fact that they will buy it sometime in the future. The seventeenth time, they make a note to buy the product. The eighteenth time, they curse their poverty for not allowing them to buy this terrific product. The nineteenth time, they count their money very carefully. The twentieth time prospects see the ad, they buy what is being offered.

Guess what? Not a whole lot has changed since 1885. Thomas Smith understood repetition. He understood getting noticed, too!

Jay Conrad Levinson, the father of *Guerrilla Marketing* and author of many guerrilla marketing books, including being my co-author for *Guerrilla Marketing in 30 Days*, stated that two out of three marketing messages are ignored. If that's true and it takes six to eight touches to your target market to motivate them to take action, then, according to Jay's theory, a target market really needs to be touched *18 to 24 times* before they will take action. Regardless of which frequency you go with, the point is that you need to repeatedly communicate your marketing message to get noticed and to stay top of mind.

There are a few more factors at work related to frequency. First, your prospects only remember a small amount of what they see and what they learn today, whether it's a marketing message or any other kind of information. You can just about bet that your marketing message will not be part of that learned material. It might be, but chances are it won't be on the first go-around.

As you know, the amount of marketing messages that prospects are hit with on a daily basis is staggering. So instead of six to eight, or 18 or 24, or 20 as Thomas Smith wrote, you are fighting for mindshare and you must get noticed from among thousands of messages—many of those repeated messages.

Successful advertisers understand the value of frequency, and so should you. I once worked with a customer who wanted to do a mailing to 5,000 people. My recommendation to her was to shelve 4,000 of the 5,000 names and mail five times to 1,000 people on her list. The costs are the same in either case, but because of the frequency of a five-time repetition of a mailing, the potential response rate would be higher than with a single mailing.

What's more, the message in those five mailings should be the same. Communicating different information to your target market each time is far less effective than delivering a repeated message. Every time your prospect gets a different message, the frequency or repetition pattern starts over.

Repetition brings familiarity. Familiarity adds to credibility and starts, builds, and maintains relationships with prospects and customers—exactly what you want to happen when you market like you mean it.

When you are connected like you are today and marketing messages interrupt you constantly, you tend to take notice and remember the descriptive stories associated with messages, not always the messages themselves. In the next chapter notice the facts, descriptions, pathways, and points of emphasis that make up remembered stories.

MARKETING TRUTH

Frequency and repetition are as important as the other key considerations of marketing: the target, the message, and the marketing vehicle you choose to get the message to the target market.

Chapter 2 / How to Survive the Marketing Message Storm

3

IT'S ALL
ABOUT
THE STORY

C HANCES ARE, YOU'VE HEARD A STORY IN THE LAST FEW MONTHS, from a friend, family member, or from the tons of media we're all subjected to on a daily basis. Chances are, too, that you have also heard some statistics of one sort or another. Which of these two types of information was easiest to remember? My bet is on the story you heard.

STORIES GET NOTICED AND REMEMBERED

Stories have existed since long before recorded history, back many thousands of years ago to at least the Lascaux caves in the mountains of southern France. Since then, stories have changed dramatically, from paintings to the printed word to movies, all the way to today's stories, which are aided by the many forms of technology. The desire to hear stories hasn't changed, nor has the longing to tell stories. Today, though, there are more stories than ever. So the challenge is standing out from this clutter. Just as important to standing out is getting remembered in this ultra-connected, interruptive world.

Consider Aesop. Aesop's fabled fables originated in pre-Christian times and were remembered, retold, and passed on without a single scrap of paper or drop of ink. People remembered Aesop's stories so well that by the time printing was invented, the details, messages, and lessons were still intact, all as a result of the years and years of storytelling.

Throughout history, storytellers became prominent. The ability to tell tales, while making them memorable, was a priceless skill. Whether biblical stories, the legend of someone's life journey, or a lesson handed down through generations of family, stories are kept alive through word-of-mouth storytelling.

Now fast forward to modern times. Consider Steve Jobs. Jobs' commencement speech at Stanford University is an example of a great story. Actually, it's the tying together of many stories into a single delivery. Jobs' story starts with him talking about being born to a young, unwed college-graduate mother and adopted by working-class parents. He attended private colleges, shacking up with friends, and eventually dropping out of school. Jobs tells the story of a calligraphy class that helped him launch the typefaces of the original Macintosh computer. His message during the Stanford speech was clear: ". . . you can't connect the dots looking forward; you can only connect them looking backwards. So you have to trust that the dots will somehow connect in your future. You have to trust in something—your gut, destiny, life, karma, whatever . . ."

Jobs' speech continued with more tales of life and death. He tells the story of being fired by Apple and his battle with cancer and in facing death. His stories became messages; and we all know that millions paid attention to his messages and remembered them. Not every marketing message needs to include a retelling of a personal journey, but interjecting a degree of humanity by drawing upon personal experiences and talking about them can give your messages power and meaning.

Nike embraces the power of the story, too. In 1970, Nike designated their executives "Corporate Storytellers" as part of their corporate culture. The stories the company leaders told ranged from recounting the company history, "the Nike story," to many tales of people simply getting things accomplished. (Think of the company's iconic "Just Do It" tagline.) By helping all their employees understand the company's past, the stories that Nike executives tell help shape the company's future. They state this at the beginning of every new employee's employment; it's ingrained in their culture. Imagine hearing the story of how Nike founder Bill Bowerman went to his workshop one day after a brainstorm session and poured shoe rubber into the family waffle iron. That was the birth of the famous Nike waffle sole. The telling of stories like this reflects "the spirit of innovation" at the shoe company, while connecting today's work to Nike's heritage and roots.

Nike's storytelling extends to the sharing and telling of the Nike story to retail distributors and salespeople. Dennis Reeder, training manager at Nike, says, "When people understand why we exist, what our foundation is, and who we are today, then they understand that all our products are still rooted in improving athletes' performance." Getting salespeople and customers to remember the Nike mission of improving performance sells more shoes.

Whether it's sharing a mission, selling shoes, or inspiring a commitment to performance, storytelling is a powerful tool that can mean the difference between extraordinary status and being just another brand. More businesses are realizing what Nike has recognized: the power of storytelling. Business communication doesn't just have to be bullet points, simple statements, or rhetorical rants. A dose of the human element, emotions, and branded thinking can result in a memorable message. As we continue to stress in this book, it's getting remembered that's such an essential component of business success. Stories build messages that people care about. Stories help people bond to messages. People remember what they care about and bond with. When you engage listeners in a powerful, entertaining, and informative story, they remember it, and many times they ask for more.

Emotions and experiences—especially personal ones—are what make a story stand out. Visit the Dr. Pepper/Snapple Group website and you can read the story of Nantucket Nectars:

Tom First and Tom Scott, known as Tom and Tom, met at Brown University in the fall of 1985. Four years later, they graduated and headed to Nantucket. That summer they started Allserve, a floating convenience store serving boats in Nantucket Harbor. The pair delivered everything from newspapers to laundry in their unmistakable red boat. Then came that fateful winter night, when the blender was pulled out and the juices mixed.

The story of that life-changing night led to the creation of the Nantucket Nectars refreshment beverage business, which was acquired by Cadbury Schweppes in 2002 and then integrated into the Plano, Texas-based Dr. Pepper/Snapple Group, a global beverage business that sells 50 beverage brands.

MARKETING TRUTH

Interject humanity and personal experiences to tell powerful stories that can transform your marketing messages.

"TOMA": TOP-OF-MIND AWARENESS

We all enjoy a good story, whether it's a novel, a movie, or simply the description of an experience shared by a friend. Stories put our whole brain to work, not just parts of it. We feel more engaged when hearing narratives and we remember them more. What gets remembered becomes top of mind.

Is there someone you know that everyone refers to as "the computer guy"? Or maybe you've heard something like, "I need to see that car-repair guy" or "You know that woman—the birthday-cake lady?" These labels stuck because these people did more than just start their job or career and get to work. They gained icon status (even locally) by creating what's known in marketing circles as *top-of-mind awareness*. When the need arises for a particular service or product, ask yourself what the first person, company, or store is that comes to mind? Whether it's a person or a business, whoever you thought of has achieved top-of-mind awareness.

Maybe you have even heard a story or experience related to these people, products, or services. The goal of marketing is for a brand to literally be at that top spot, right where all the thought of a need or a want passes through.

Stories create buzz. The more buzz about a product or service, obviously the more awareness there is about that brand. And the more awareness there is, the higher the probability of being in that top-of-mind position. Your customers and prospects are making choices, preferences, and buying decisions every day. Very often, these decisions are made as a result of what comes to mind first. Think about your favorite watering hole, restaurant, go-to place for electronics and gifts. The key to getting noticed and talked about is learning how to catapult your brand into your customer's mind, preferably at the top of that mind. Marketing, building awareness, and creating buzz are all made up of many factors working together synergistically. Getting that label (and the top-of-mind placement that goes with it) starts with making an initial announcement. If it's a business, you use a press release to announce a grand opening. Thought-provoking information that teaches and shares can place messages and brands at the top of mind.

Consider these characteristics when creating thought leadership that helps create top-of-mind awareness:

! Do your thoughts advance a concept or idea?
! Are your thoughts actionable?
! How commercially relevant are your thoughts?
! Do you have data and research that backs up your thoughts?
! Is your point of view new and fresh?
! Does your information offer a new insight?
! Can your thought leadership influence others?
! Will recipients of your thought leadership change the way they think or act about something?

Still, sometimes this is not enough to create the necessary buzz to reach that top-of-mind position in your target market's mind. So what do you do then? Think of the battle for top-of-mind awareness as a journey from deep inside your heart to the top of your head. In other words, you need your customers, prospects, friends, and associates to connect with you emotionally and to love you. Loving something will immediately land in that top-of-mind space.

Creating and sustaining top-of-mind awareness is a long-term process, not a one-time marketing event. You have to think in terms of a "process" because, according to Chilton Research, more than 60 percent of your potential customers are waiting seven to 12 months to make a choice, a preference, or a final purchasing decision. Because of that, you need to have a long-term plan for top-of-mind awareness. In marketing, consistency is a foundational concept. Staying fresh, interesting, and relevant over the long-term will contribute to staying top of mind.

If you want to be top of mind, you also naturally have to put your message where you'll find the customers you're trying to reach. One of the dangers of mass marketing, in fact, is missing your target market and hitting those who aren't your target. Let the world know that you exist and what you have to say. This also relates to talking with the prospect in mind. We say it often in this book, but remember to talk from the perspective of the prospect or customer, answering the question, "What's in it for me, the prospect?" That means you better have something fresh, relevant, and interesting to say that also translates into value for those receiving your message. What you find interesting and relevant might not be what your customers want to hear. Think about being valuable to your prospect. Think about being informative.

If you're wondering whether social sharing on platforms like Facebook, Twitter, and Pinterest contributes to top-of-mind awareness, the answer is a resounding yes. Since social sharing is done in communities of like-minded people with similar interests, the journey to top of mind can be quick. Social communities made up of similar people wanting

---

MARKETING TRUTH

Creating and sustaining top-of-mind awareness is a long-term process, not a one-time marketing event.

---

similar, targeted messages are typically smaller and more efficient for purposes of communication, too. Social sharing also tends to be done on a more consistent basis; and status updates, sharing of news, photos, and information, and blog comments are likelier to get noticed. As a marketer, you can create and plan an editorial calendar that outlines a schedule of communication with your customers that will ensure consistency.

JARED: SUBWAY®

When talking about getting noticed and getting talked about—and especially getting remembered—the story of Jared and his association with the Subway® sandwich chain rises to the top of the list. Millions have heard his story. Millions have bought Subway sandwiches. There are now almost 41,000 Subway restaurants in 103 countries, and that empire didn't happen without the help of a grossly overweight Indiana University freshman, starting back in 1998.

How did Jared get noticed? Why do you know his story and possibly buy Subway sandwiches? And why does the Jared buzz continue, more than 15 years later? Let's take a look: Jared Fogle was a 425-pound college student who was so fat that he couldn't fit through doorways or squeeze into car seats. He chose college classes by testing classroom seats to see if could maneuver his frame into them. One day he noticed a sign at the Subway near where he lived. It was promoting the restaurant's "7 under 6" menu: seven submarine sandwiches with six grams of fat or less. Jared decided to give it a try. Many diets had come and gone, leading to no lasting success for Jared. That day he tried the infamous turkey sub for lunch; he went back for dinner and had the veggie sub. Since he liked the sandwiches, he continued the same regimen for the next year. It led to a weight loss of close to 50 pounds in one year; Jared was hooked. He had the beginning of a story, which is the first component of getting noticed.

Shortly after Jared started his new sub-eating lifestyle, a former dorm mate of Jared's wrote an article about Jared's weight loss for the *Indiana Daily Student*, the university's student-run newspaper. It was a front-page story titled "From Thick to Thin" and it covered Jared's dramatic weight loss from eating submarine sandwiches, including dramatic before-and-after photos. *Men's Health* magazine took notice and included a mention of his sandwich diet in an article called "Stupid Diets . . . that Work!" Before long, a Subway franchisee in nearby Chicago had picked up the idea and presented it to Subway's advertising agency. Soon the agency was on to a new ad campaign focused on healthy lifestyle—a message that took over all of Subway's marketing. It was a marketing masterpiece that took advantage of one of Americans' biggest concerns: how to live healthfully, lose weight, and still enjoy meals.

Subway got thousands of letters from consumers inspired by Jared and the healthy weight loss he accomplished with the help of Subway. A phenomenon was born. Despite the fact that Jared's story has been told by countless media outlets, he continued to be an inspiration for thousands who'd heard about his incredible weight-loss success. Word spread. People talked, shared, and wanted to learn more, which continued to fuel the marketing fire. Jared Fogle is still an international celebrity, even an icon, and he's still appearing in TV commercials the world over, advocating for healthier lifestyles. Becoming an icon of *anything* is the ultimate marketing achievement. Robin Lee Allen, executive editor of *Nation's Restaurant News,* said it best: "Jared gave Subway the health halo before any of us even knew the term. Nobody else has struck on a Jared."

Here are eight keys to making your marketing messages stick in people's minds, Subway Jared-style:

1. *People can identify with a regular guy.* Jared is very likable, not like other icons or celebrities, and he appears to be very approachable. It's clear that he had the same challenge (being overweight) as nearly three-fourths of Americans, which made him highly relatable.

2. *Find the person with the story.* Many brands, companies, and causes have that one person to whom people relate on an emotional basis because of their story. It might be a story of success or survival. Emotion and inspiration motivate others to take action, another ultimate objective in marketing.

3. *Keep the story simple.* What Jared did was something anyone could do. It was simple, not elaborate, and didn't require lots of training or instruction. People will take more notice of something they understand easily.

4. *Maximize the visuals.* Just like Jared, you, your friends, and your family members probably all have pants that you can't fit in to. Jared's 58-inch waist pants became the visual touchstone of his journey—and the place he never wanted to return to. When you see the huge pants that Jared used to wear you remember them and are likely to feel inspired, too.

5. *Keep the message relevant.* More than 70 percent of Americans 20 and older are overweight, so anything related to a healthier lifestyle is relevant and likely to be paid attention to by a large percentage of these people, most of whom want to live more healthfully. What Jared did mattered to a lot of people, so they were very willing to pay attention.

6. *Keep the focus on the story.* We've talked at length already in this book about the power of the story. That's because stories are engaging. Jared's time at Subway, starting from that first sandwich on Day One, is a journey told to you in the style of a story. It's easy to trace his steps and hear the ups and downs, the emotions, the challenges, and his successes; all important components to a good story. It was also a fun story. All these things contribute to the story being told again and again by Jared, his advocates, and many other people. It gets talked about.

7. *Don't forget surprise and intrigue.* From the get-go, Jared's story had one key surprise factor: that it's possible to lose weight by eating fast food. It didn't dawn on Subway or the ad agency at first but when the idea was tested with customers, it was a hit. That's surprising, and it caught audiences off guard.

8. *Don't overdo the hype.* Sensationalism was not necessary with Jared's story. There was no need to pump up any of the factors in this tale, because the real facts, with a real person in real time, were plenty.

So Subway got noticed, remembered, and talked about, but did it help the business beyond that? It sure did. Subway more than tripled its U.S. sales, to $11.5 billion in 2011, from about the year before the start of Jared's journey, according to *Nation's Restaurant News.* Subway has grown to more than 38,000 locations and has more locations in the U.S.

> # MARKETING TRUTH
>
> *Becoming an icon creates buzz that's built on sharing stories that people want to hear, remember, and experience.*

and globally than McDonald's. Restaurant researcher Malcolm Knapp reported "Subway generated the perception that it's a healthy place to eat through Jared, and it stuck. That's a very powerful tool. You don't hear people saying that they can eat healthy at McDonald's."

INSPIRATIONAL: RACHAEL RAY AND PAULA DEEN

Rachael Ray got noticed by telling her story of satisfying a need and doing what she liked to do best (while making ends meet in the meantime). As you read this section, think to yourself, what story about you or the brand you're promoting exemplifies what you like to do best? What part of your story might others want to hear? What about your experience would benefit others?

Ray may call herself a "hick from the sticks," but she has become an industry. One of her first jobs when she moved to New York City was working the candy counter at Macy's. From there she was eventually promoted to manager of Macy's Fresh Foods department. Ray learned a lot about gourmet foods at this job, and she used that knowledge to help open and manage a prestigious gourmet foods marketplace. Eventually, after moving back to upstate New York, she managed Mister Brown's Pub at The Sagamore, a hotel on Lake George. From there, she became a buyer at Cowan & Lobel, a gourmet food market in Albany. To help sell more groceries, Ray started a cooking class called "30-Minute Meals" to help customers who told her they were stretched for time, or didn't want to cook; as a food buyer she saw too many customers buying ready-made meals instead of cooking for themselves. She also made up a set of cards of "30-Minute Meals" and handed them out, while telling customers that if they had 30 minutes to wait for a pizza to be delivered that they could also spend 30 minutes to cook something at home.

Ray's class became so popular that a local TV station offered her a weekly spot. At the same time, she decided to put some of her recipes into a cookbook. Combining her infectious personality, trademarked expressions, and ease in front of the camera, people took notice. First it was Albany's CBS affiliate, who approached Ray about doing a weekly segment for the evening news called "30-Minute Meals"; the show received multiple regional Emmys. Soon the network TV stations came calling; they'd taken notice.

Next, Ray's book got into the hands of NBC's *Today Show* and Ray found herself next to Al Roker, demonstrating quick and easy ways to make chicken and dumpling soup. She was a hit, and the next day, the Food Network signed her to a large contract. Ray's simple 30-minute meals and bubbly personality were so popular that she became noticed as a celebrity chef. Her friendly, outgoing personality and simple meals continue to get noticed, building her TV viewership even more. Getting noticed is typically a result of tenacity, and Ray was helped along by her lighthearted attitude, a good camera presence, and giving people what they want.

Paula Deen's story is very similar. Deen moved her catering company to a small restaurant in a Best Western motel in Savannah, Georgia, and opened her first restaurant, The Lady and Sons, with her sons Bobby and Jamie. The restaurant was a hit, and the popularity of Deen and her cooking led to her first cookbook, *The Lady and Sons Savannah Country Cookbook*. This gave her fans the opportunity to try Deen's recipes at home and led to her first TV appearance on QVC to market her books and restaurant. Deen had a warmth about her and a friendly Southern personality that made her a natural for TV. She soon premiered *Paula's Home Cooking* on the Food Network, sending her on the way to superstardom.

The Rachael Ray and Paula Deen stories work to inspire, to motivate, to attract attention, and to get remembered and talked about. Consider the following:

! Inspiring people with experiences and ideas can help launch businesses, turn ideas into reality, and propel wishes to come true.

! These and similar stories encourage readers to pursue their dreams, in spite of setbacks and the demands of everyday life.

Stories like these encourage us all to find happiness, success, and fulfillment.

! Readers of the Ray and Deen stories feel that they can identify with these personalities' early challenges, their pursuit of a dream, and the hope for success that comes from hard work and perseverence.

When you drill down to what got noticed, remembered, and talked about for both Rachael Ray and Paula Deen, it was their warmth and personality. People generally respond well to those qualities and end up liking those who display them. Ray and Deen are personable, each in their own way. Their stories talk about that and that gets noticed.

Sometimes if a marketing message, story, or tactic seems awkward, out of the mainstream, or extreme, it might be worth doing to get noticed. Get ready to get way out and borderline on weird in the next chapter as we investigate some wild, wacky, and bold workings of marketing.

MARKETING TRUTH

Getting noticed is the result of tenacity, a lighthearted attitude, a good camera presence, giving people what they want, warmth, and personality.

4

WILD, WACKY, AND BOLD: USING HUMOR TO GET NOTICED

ADDING HUMOR TO YOUR CONTENT IS ONE THING THAT WILL surely get your marketing messaging noticed. After all, your customers like to laugh as much as you do. Both customers and prospects continually face a constant onslaught of social media, video, email, marketing messages, and more, both on- and offline. Adding a touch of humor will help to capture your target's attention. It's a fact that content that's laughed at is shared more often and is more memorable than "straight" messaging.

Laughter is a reaction. Reactions are engagement. Engagement lifts the awareness of a brand and typically gets it talked about and remembered. Since the very first day that some product or service was marketed and sold, marketers and sellers have understood that sex and humor are effective topics to break through the mind and marketing clutter. We all know that humor sells. Just look at the highest-ranked Super Bowl commercials every year. Those that are funny are talked about at the water cooler the following day. Humorous commercials get ranked high in all the polls. Funny ads are watched over and over and no one seems to mind the repetition.

Studies have shown that university students increase retention and pay greater attention if instructors add humor to their teaching. This is more evidence that making someone laugh is a way to get people to not only enjoy themselves, but to pay attention, remember, and maybe even talk about your product or service. It also substantiates that humor is more memorable than dry facts, statistics, and lecture points. The best teachers usually offer humorous anecdotes, crack jokes, and create stories and context that make boring topics more interesting and therefore easier to learn. Getting a person's attention is the critical first step to getting them to remember (learn) important information. In marketing terms, using humor will grab the attention of a customer or potential customer and aid in creating that top-of-mind awareness for your message or brand long after the message is delivered.

Southwest Airlines uses humor all the time. They say they do it to get people to pay attention to safety information before and during the flight. And passengers are more likely to do so, especially when compared to the dry presentations by other airlines. Although Southwest was first, other airlines are starting to use videos spiced with humor to get people to pay attention to the safety guidelines. Here are some examples from flight attendants and crew of how Southwest uses in-flight humor to get passengers to listen up:

"Good news! It looks like we will be arriving in Copenhagen just as we had planned. This means we have to end this journey as we started it, with seatbacks and tray tables in an upright position. This of course serves no purpose, but makes the pilots very happy.

"If the cupcake-looking plastic things drop down in front of you, stop screaming, let go of your neighbor, and put it over your mouth.

"We'll be dimming the lights in the cabin. Pushing the light-bulb button will turn your reading light on. However, pushing the flight-attendant button will not turn your flight attendant on.

"Your seat cushions can be used for flotation. In the event of an emergency water landing, please paddle to shore and take them with our compliments.

"We've reached our cruising altitude now, and I'm turning off the seat belt sign. I'm switching to autopilot, too, so I can come back there and visit with all of you for the rest of the flight.

"If you smoke in this airplane, the FAA will fine you $2,000 [pause] and at those prices, you might as well fly Delta!"

If you heard any of these you would take notice, right? You would probably laugh too, but you'd also definitely pay attention and you might even tell someone about it after you got off the plane.

Year after year, and for a long time, the airline has experienced growth in sales and profits. Southwest's attitude about humor continues to help bring the airline outstanding success. It always ranks high in punctuality and quick baggage delivery and low on customer complaints.

Humor, in fact, is taken very seriously at Southwest. The airline's corporate philosophy and company culture are built on the fact that humor will help people thrive and relieve tension. It's even part of the Southwest mission statement and the chairman lives out the philosophy, summarized in four simple points:

1. Lighten up.
2. Be more playful.
3. Don't take yourself too seriously.
4. Remember to have fun!

Whether you are Southwest Airlines, a local small business, or an ecommerce site, you may find that plenty of people pay attention to you and share your content simply by adding humor.

Southwest is not the only company using humor, of course. Remember the Budweiser frogs, or the donkey that wanted to be a Clydesdale? What about the AFLAC duck, sometimes intermingled with baseball humorist Yogi Berra? Just watch commercials during the Super Bowl and tally up funny commercials versus non-funny commercials (there will be lots more of the former). Studies show that younger generations prefer information with humor. Instead of the nightly news, they're watching videos on YouTube or Vimeo, or tuning in to *The Colbert Report* or *The Daily Show with Jon Stewart*.

How many times do you see social media postings that are about nothing? Comedian Jerry Seinfeld mastered the art of "nothing" with humor. He turned everyday life into a litany of funny quips and satire that was watched over and over. As Mark Twain eloquently said, "Humor is mankind's greatest blessing." Use this blessing in your marketing and you will gain the mindshare you want.

MARKETING TRUTH

The use of humor will grab the attention of a customer or potential customer and will aid in creating that top-of-mind awareness for your message or brand long after the message is delivered.

KMART: SHIP MY PANTS

I'm here to tell you that sophomoric humor gets attention. What makes a video go viral are often the stupid, obnoxious, extreme, crazy, stunt-laden, and hilarious things. Those are some of the adjectives used to describe a commercial by Kmart in which the chain promoted their free shipping option. When Kmart shoppers couldn't find something in one of their stores, a Kmart associate would offer to find it at Kmart.com and ship it to the customer free of charge. Given this premise and a juvenile play on words, a viral ad was born.

Kmart promoted the new shipping benefit by letting people know that it was OK to "ship their pants," and just about anything else they wanted to "ship." The ad took off, full of plenty of "ship" references, as you might guess. The entire commercial's script has various people saying "ship" or "shipped" (instead of the more vulgar s-word). People of all types, including family members, a child, a Kmart employee, an elderly couple, and other customers shopping in the store are featured in the ad. An edgy sense of humor took over and got noticed and millions of potential shoppers found out that Kmart offered free shipping for members of their "Shop Your Way" program when any product the shoppers wanted wasn't in stock in the store.

News networks such as CNN's HLN and social media everywhere reported on the controversial, attention-getting ad, and the video of the ad on Kmart's YouTube channel soared to more than 20 million views. MediaPost.com's advertising columnist Barbara Lippert wrote that people should never underestimate the power of a good "doody" joke. "It's fourth-grade humor, but it makes you laugh," she says. The play on words throughout the ad is so simple, but so effective. In this case, hilariousness got noticed.

In case you missed it, here is the script:

Ship my pants, right here. You're kidding! Ship my pants. You can ship your pants right here. Did you hear that? I can ship my pants for free. Whoa! I just may ship my pants. Yes, ship your pants. Billy, you can ship your pants too. I can't wait to ship my pants, Dad. I just shipped my pants, and it is very convenient. Very convenient. I just shipped my drawers. I just shipped my nightie. I just shipped my bed!

That isn't the only surprising ad that Kmart has done; they created an equally noticeable commercial titled "Big Gas Savings." The premise is the same (it sounds as if they're swearing, but they're not). Blending the last letter of the first word ("big") and the first letter of the second word ("gas") leads to another curse-sounding phrase. The actors continue their playful puns throughout the commercial, all the way to the end, when bystanders marvel at a "big gas truck" and a "big gas man" as the ad reveals a big fuel tanker driven by a noticeably tall man. The ad not only got noticed, it got its message across nicely. That message was that a customer could save 30 cents per gallon at select Kmart gas stations by becoming a member of the "Shop Your Way" rewards program offered by Kmart and Sears.

Chapter 4 / Wild, Wacky, and Bold: Using Humor to Get Noticed

In commercials for Super Bowl XLV, Teleflora included singer Faith Hill helping her male sound engineer write a card for his girlfriend's Valentine's Day flowers. Hill tried to help her friend get in touch with his sentimental side, to help him channel his true emotions into words—but to no avail. His final card to his girlfriend? "Dear Kim, your rack is unreal." The ad got noticed, the acting was understated and believable, the joke wasn't forced, and the viewing audience learned about Teleflora. Mission accomplished.

Then there was the enthusiastic ad campaign for the Mini Cooper car using suggestive vocabulary to catch viewers' attention. Mini Cooper took the risqué route with their new Super Bowl commercial, "Cram It in the Boot!" while showcasing a game show-style TV show called *Cram It in the Boot*. In the ad a sequin-clad hostess makes a suggestive motion during the opening of the faux game show while a passionate British host asks an innocent contestant, "Have you ever crammed it in the boot before?" After admitting that no, he has never crammed it in the boot, he's encouraged to run around the set, finding large boxes and containers to shove in the back of a Mini's "boot." ("Boot" is the British slang word for the trunk of a car, as we know it in the U.S.) Mini Cooper took advantage of this British/ American language barrier to make a sassy reference for their Super Bowl stage.

By now you have seen that many brands that understand their target markets can apply a little imagination and use humor effectively to get noticed and get remembered. It is a formula that works and one that should be used more. Humor is social by nature; people share funny stories all the time. It's no secret or surprise that the most viral online videos are those that do the best job of making you laugh. A humorous

---

MARKETING TRUTH

Brands that understand their target markets can effectively apply imagination and humor to get noticed and remembered. It's a formula that works and one that should be used more often.

---

brand is a confident brand, and a confident brand is in demand—and gets noticed.

CHURCH SIGNS

For the past 20 years, Reverend Paul Sinclair has put up humorous, thought-provoking, attention-getting signs outside his church in Willesden Green, North London. Rev. Sinclair achieves his goal of grabbing the attention of passersby, the media, potential church members, and devout parishioners. Each sign has a witty and thought-provoking message, spreading peace and love in a wonderfully unconventional way. Regardless of religion, his mission is to celebrate life and laughter but only after he grabs attention and gets noticed.

Church signs have a celebrated and storied history. From the community message board to a platform to encourage, they have stood for many centuries. Churches realize that sometimes you need a sense of humor and a sense of community to get messages across. The church road sign has often offered direction and pearls of wisdom to travelers. Church signs can be thought of as mini roadside sermons for our on-the-go times.

Church signs are so popular that there are now websites devoted to this method of communication. Many books have been written to showcase favorites, creating "church sign buzz." It's almost to a point where you can't drive by a church today without making an effort to see what the next message to the faithful (and even the non-faithful) might be. Communication and buzz are essential in all of marketing. You can learn both of these from your observation of church signs.

There is no doubt that church signs have a promotional mission, and as with any promotion, getting noticed comes first. Church signs act like a miniature billboard to promote inspiration and faith. Church leaders use their signs as a vehicle for getting their congregation known in the community and connecting faith with daily life, community events, and humor. Some signs are humorous, some are encouraging, some are wise, some aim to be convincing. All are designed to turn scant seconds of drive-by time into active spiritual awareness. Let's look at some head-turning examples:

A sunrise is God's way of saying "lighten up."

Where will you be spending eternity: smoking or non-smoking?

Love is grand. Divorce is 20 grand.

Now open Sundays!

Seven days without prayer makes one weak.

The Ten Commandments are not multiple choice.

Looking for a lifeguard? Ours walks on water.

Forbidden fruit creates many jams.

Under the same management for more than 2,000 years.

Speak well of your enemies; you made them.

Here are a few best practices for what makes an effective promotional message, whether you're a church leader, a business owner, or an entrepreneur:

! As with a billboard, a local sign gives you only a few seconds to grab someone's attention and communicate the whole message. Phrases should be short, with letters big enough to be read upon passing by. Quick and succinct are the keys to effective communication.

! New, fresh messages get attention more than stale messages left up for long periods of time.

! Keep in mind your purpose: Announcements can be made but will be more effective in other communication vehicles.

! Positive sells, humor sells, inspiration sells. You can't bore people into buying your message.

Just like other types of marketing, an attention-getting church sign is a promotional tool that should work around the clock.

MARKETING TRUTH

You need a sense of humor and community to get messages across.

VETERINARY SIGNS

Churches aren't the only businesses trying to get noticed, of course. Marquee signs offer a marketing touch point for any business or organization that takes advantage of its "front and center" display. Take the Eau Gallie Veterinary Hospital, in Melbourne, Florida. They are getting noticed on every drive-by thanks to their creative messages.

Would the signs below turn your head? (Keep in mind that these are veterinarians who are passionate about controlling the animal birth rate.)

> Neutering Your Pets Makes Them Less Nuts
> Live Nude Dogs! Free Lap Dances!
> If You Don't Talk to Your Cat About Catnip, Who Will?
> The Only Balls Your Dog Needs Are the Ones He Fetches
> We Like Big Mutts and We Cannot Lie!
> No Hump Wednesdays. 10% Off Spaying and Neutering

MARKETING TRUTH

Marquee signs offer a marketing touch point for any business or organization that wants to take advantage of a "front and center" display at their business.

FUNNY BAR SIGNS

In addition to church signs and vet signs, bars and pubs offer great inspiration for effective signage. You see them everywhere, but you probably don't notice them: those chalkboard easel signs in front of retail establishments, bars, and restaurants. You see them, but unless the message grabs your attention you don't take notice, exactly like other marketing messages coming at you daily. But if the message on the sign stands out, you will take notice. Chalkboard signs generally flag a passerby that a bar, restaurant, or shop is open or some other mundane message. But a witty, clever, extreme, in-your-face, funny message stands out. Customers take note and are enticed off their walking path and into the establishment behind the chalkboard.

Let's take a look at some of the more successful pub messages:

> You can't drink all day if you don't start in the morning.
>
> Is everything OK? If yes, come in and have a drink. If no, come in and have a drink.
>
> Free Booze and False Advertising
>
> Whiskey is sunlight held together by water.
>
> We're airing LIVE the XXX Olympiad, Featuring GIRLS Volleyball and Fencing. (On this sign the words LIVE, XXX, and GIRLS are much larger than the other words; you get the point.)
>
> Buy 1 Beer for the Price of 2 and Get the Second One Free
>
> Alcohol: Because no good story started with someone eating a salad
>
> Guys: No Shirt, No Service; Girls: No Shirt, No Charge
>
> Roses Are Red, Beer Is Great, Poems Are Hard, BEER!
>
> Free Air Guitar with Every Pint

I guarantee that you will tell someone about one of these messages and have a laugh—and remember the message.

MARKETING TRUTH

Clever and funny sayings and messages get noticed and bring customers in the front door.

SOMETIMES YOU JUST HAVE TO ASK TO GET NOTICED

Sometimes in order to get noticed you simply have to ask. As the old proverb goes, "Be careful what you ask for; you just might get it!" That's exactly what happened to Michael Pollack, a Vanderbilt University student who was attending "Billy Joel: An Evening of Questions and Answers and a Little Bit of Music," a symposium with the singer. Pollack asked Joel if he could accompany him in a rendition of "New York State of Mind." Joel agreed and Pollack beelined it to the stage before Joel could change his mind. The duet was a musical home run. Joel was clearly impressed and finished by telling the audience, "Michael Pollack: Remember that name." Not only did Pollack get noticed, the audience's likelihood of remembering the talented student was fueled when Joel uttered the word "remember."

The day after the impromptu show, Pollack appeared on the *Today Show* to tell his story of getting noticed. Michael Pollack's wildest dream had come true. He had had the courage to ask Billy Joel exactly what he wanted. Pollack wanted a chance to get noticed—and it worked. Michael Pollack's life may have changed forever as a result of simply asking for what he wanted: Music industry giant BMI took notice and signed Pollack to a song-writing contract and now he's on his way to being remembered and talked about. All he did was ask. All he did was "wow" the person he asked to notice him.

MARKETING TRUTH

To get noticed sometimes you just have to ask.

OUTRAGEOUS GETS NOTICED

Consider the city that renamed itself as a domain name. Halfway, Oregon, is a town within four miles of the 45th parallel, which makes it halfway between the equator and the North Pole. *The New York Times* described the town as a sleepy village and a farming and ranching community halfway between Pine and Cornucopia, Oregon, "tucked away in the shadow of the snowy Wallowa Mountains in eastern Oregon's sagebrush country, hard by the Idaho border." According to Wikipedia, the 2000 census reported the population of Halfway as 337. The city used outrageousness to get noticed in late 1999 when it renamed itself "Half.com." At the time, Half.com was an ecommerce startup.

The town of Halfway, Oregon, wasn't looking to be renamed or soliciting for a sponsor, but a new web startup called Half.com *was* looking to get noticed somehow. As Joshua Kopelman, Half.com's CEO, explained it, the company wanted "recognition as out-of-the-box thinkers." In

Chapter 4 / Wild, Wacky, and Bold: Using Humor to Get Noticed

exchange, the startup offered the renamed city $110,000 and computers for its schools, along with other financial incentives.

Truth or Consequences, New Mexico

Half.com wasn't the only city that used its naming rights to get noticed and get attention. In the 1950s, there was a TV/radio quiz show that aired on NBC called *Truth or Consequences*. In later years the show was hosted by the famous Bob Barker, but the original host was Ralph Edwards. Ralph wanted higher ratings and he wanted to get noticed and to create a buzz about the show. So Ralph announced that he would broadcast the show from the first town that changed their name to the name of the show. He got a taker and Truth or Consequences, New Mexico, was born and continues today, mostly affectionately known as T or C, New Mexico, with a population of just over 7,000. You've heard of it because it's talked about and associated with a game show that got talked about. This naming game may have set a precedent. Radio personality Don Imus sold naming rights for his nonprofit New Mexico cattle ranch for kids with cancer to *Reader's Digest* and is now called Reader's Digest, New Mexico.

You don't need to rename your town to use outrageous tactics effectively as a marketer. Here are some ideas that are outrageous, but not as elaborate, that will help you get noticed and talked about:

- ！ *Make them laugh, make them cry, make them mad, make them love.* You've read it here and you will hear it again. Tie things to emotions and you increase the probability of getting noticed.

- ！ *Stage a public event.* I once witnessed a company that had protesters (staged by the company) in front of the corporate office, protesting "Great Customer Service." This "positive" protest was way different, outrageous, and definitely noticed!

- ！ *Weird works.* We're all weird in our way, but being quirky stands out among all the "normal" content we're inundated with. People also share weird content, usually because it's unique and unusual.

- ！ *Aim for the uplifting and moving.* Creating an emotional connection with any content will certainly be remembered. Try to invoke emotions by telling a story and tugging on the heartstrings.

All of these are just the tip of the "outrageous" iceberg. If your message, content, or delivery is shocking, extraordinary, or unconventional, these are qualities that will catch people's attention and be talked about.

MARKETING TRUTH

Marketing messages and content that are outrageous, shocking, extraordinary, and unconventional catch people's attention and will be talked about.

FLASH MOBS GET NOTICED

What started as a social experiment by senior editor Bill Wasik of *Harper's* magazine in 2003 has turned into a pop culture phenomenon. Flash mobs continue to be popular, serving a multitude of purposes: marriage proposals, reunions, birthday celebrations, company and product announcements, and more. More advertisers are using the unconventional approach of flash mobs to grab attention.

Simply put, a flash mob is a large group of people who gather to perform together an act that appears to be happening spontaneously, usually to draw attention to something and usually in a public space. Sometimes they are done for fun; other times they are done to raise awareness of something. The point to of a flash mob is to get attention, get talked about, and most of all, be remembered. One flash mob recreated the famous fake orgasm scene from *When Harry Met Sally,* with 20 women in Katz's Deli, where the scene was shot for the film. This was staged without the knowledge of the restaurant (though the employees seemed to love it) by Improv Everywhere, a New York City "prank collective" that causes scenes of chaos and joy in public places. Created in August 2001 by Charlie Todd, Improv Everywhere has executed more than 100 missions involving tens of thousands of "undercover agents."

Why do flash mobs work? Why do they get noticed, and most of all why do people talk about them? There are six factors involved:

1. *Surprise!* Nothing gets people to pay attention faster than when they're caught off guard. A flash mob catches people unaware and it's usually exciting, uplifting, and often in your face. Those around a flash mob have to stop, listen, and take notice.

2. *The viral effect.* Once you see a flash mob you will tell someone; that is nearly guaranteed. You can't keep quiet about it. You will tell your friends, family, and co-workers in person, by phone, or on social media. You will post pictures and videos on Vine and YouTube, all contributing to the viral nature of the buzz surrounding flash mobs.

3. *PR.* Typically media of one kind or another (professional or amateur) will show up to take notice of a flash mob. To a reporter, editor, or producer a flash mob is an ideal human interest story. Human interest stories are usually fun, lighthearted, and stimulating.

4. *Unconventional tactics.* Flash mobs achieve conventional marketing goals, such as building brand awareness, but by unconventional attention-grabbing tactics. Like guerrilla marketing, this kind of marketing approach shows your prospects that you're a thought leader and progressive. Inspire and entertain your customers with your sense of adventure and out-of-the-box thinking; they'll look at your business as a leader in the marketplace and one with a sense of creativity and innovation.

5. *Increased prospect "touches."* The event itself, media coverage, and the ensuing buzz created by people talking about the flash mob mean that new prospects will be touched. Prospects turn into supporters, then into paying customers. Flash mobs that are talked about also help with the age-old marketing goal of staying top-of-mind in terms of awareness in your customers' minds.

MARKETING TRUTH

Flash mobs have entertainment value, show artistic expression, and convey messages.

6. *Getting talked about.* Once you witness a flash mob, you won't forget it and you won't stop talking about it. You may tell many people. Once you talk about it, others will do the same, spreading word quicker than wildfire.

Flash mobs can be a surefire way to get attention and get talked about.

MEN IN KILTS

A Vancouver-based window cleaning company, Men in Kilts, has taken a worn-out, commoditized category of business and made it interesting, fresh, and relevant. Men in Kilts dresses their male employees in a bright plaid Scottish kilt and a T-shirt that says "No Peeking," then sends them up a ladder to clean windows. The idea for the T-shirt's message came from the mind of Nicholas Brand, a second-generation Scotsman in Richmond, British Columbia, who took the idea, developed it, and made a thriving company out of it. "In 2002, after a night of spit-balling business concepts with friends (and perhaps downing a pint or two), Brand began cleaning windows in the Vancouver area clad in a black golf shirt, steel-toed boots, knee-high socks and the tartan of the Wallace clan, hand-stitched by his wife," said one report.

Brand's cheeky concept took hold and by 2006 he had brought on board a business partner who helped push the window-cleaning, pressure-washing, and gutter-cleaning service to the heights of success. Men in Kilts points out on their website that they started "with just $500, a rusty old Honda, and one hand-sewn kilt." Today, they're the largest window- and exterior-cleaning company in Canada. Others wanted part of the action so the company expanded, launching franchises in both Canada and the U.S. The company is living (or is it climbing?) proof that interesting, fresh, and relevant ideas are worth paying for. Add to that clever and funny, and you have a differentiated message in a cluttered world. Men in Kilts epitomizes a new definition of value—and that gets attention.

There are a few marketing lessons to be gleaned from Men in Kilts. First, think back to your target market. Women are the largest purchasers of home services, including window cleaning; this is true in the corporate world as well. So it was no coincidence that Brand knew who he was pursuing as his target customer when naming his business. That focus got them attention right from the start. In today's world of the empowered consumer, people want to do business with a brand that has personality. The days of the stuffed-shirt corporation are gone. Personality gets attention and keeps customers, and keeping customers is just as important as trying to get new ones. Find a cause, a brand, or a mission you believe in and get behind it.

It's worth noting that Men in Kilts also doesn't advertise in the traditional sense. Word-of-mouth takes over; customers come to them. People take notice because of the humor and the fact that no one else is doing what they are doing. In the world of cluttered marketing messages, any time a brand can make people smile or laugh, they stand to gain. Smiling and laughing are contagious actions, as we've said already, and contagious actions become viral. And virality will propel your business.

MARKETING TRUTH

Interesting, fresh, and relevant is valuable, and clever and funny will give you a differentiated message in a cluttered world.

RED BULL EXTREME SKYDIVER: FELIX BAUMGARTNER

Red Bull took getting attention to a new level. Their tagline, "Red Bull Gives You Wings," was the foundation of their sponsorship of extreme skydiver Felix Baumgartner. Baumgartner was the first human to break the sound barrier, in a 24-mile space jump that shattered the existing record for the highest-altitude skydive. The event, called "Red Bull Stratos," was sponsored by Red Bull Energy Drink. All the buzz, marketing, and messaging conformed to that tagline. The space jump on that November 2012 day gave Red Bull roughly eight million viewers watching live coverage, online and on TV, of the feat (and Red Bull's logo), not to mention all the water cooler talk, social media buzz, and talk that continues today, many months afterwards. This will surely be talked about for years to come and will most likely continue to be associated with Red Bull. "The sponsorship transcended sports and entertainment into pop culture, hitting new consumers that Red Bull does not usually capture, and on a global scale," said Ben Sturner, president and CEO of Leverage Agency, a sports, entertainment, and media marketing company. "The value for Red Bull is in the tens of millions of dollars of global exposure, and Red Bull Stratos will continue to be talked about and passed along socially for a very long time."

Ask just about anyone in marketing to name a brand they admire, and you'll inevitably hear about Coca-Cola, Budweiser, Disney, and Apple. These days there's likely to be a newcomer: Red Bull. The drink, created by Austrian entrepreneur Dietrich Mateschitz, is now considered a force in its beverage category, and it's also a force in marketing land. Whether it is their Red Bull can-adorned Mini Cooper car, sports team ownerships, the Red Bull Records label, or an extreme sports stunt, the marketing of getting noticed has made the brand a notable household name.

The Red Bull Stratos idea was conceived in 2005 with the goal of transcending "human limits that have existed for 50 years." A secondary goal was also very evident: getting attention for the Red Bull brand. The freefall from so far above the earth was difficult for many reasons: Temperatures at that altitude are well below freezing; too little oxygen is available at that height to breathe properly; and there was also a risk that Baumgartner would go into an uncontrollable spin, causing his body's blood to centrifuge away from the organs. Any of these on its own could cause his death. All of these risks also attracted more attention to this feat, of course.

The missions—not only to set a new record in freefall and skydiving, but also to test human limits and provide medical and scientific advancements—were accomplished. But the mission to raise awareness of the Red Bull brand to even greater heights was also accomplished. Fans monitored and flocked to both the company's branded Facebook page and to the Red Bull Stratos Facebook page. On the day of the jump, the Stratos page posts generated more than 900,000 interactions, including more than 83,000 shares. Red Bull's Facebook photo of Baumgartner after the historic jump garnered almost 216,000 Likes, 10,000 comments, and more than 29,000 shares within 40 minutes of being posted. Besides being aired on YouTube, the Stratos event was shown by more than 40 TV stations and

130 digital outlets, while half of Twitter's trending topics worldwide were related to Red Bull Stratos. The jump broke five freefalling and skydiving records, according to officials at Guinness World Records, including the first human to break the sound barrier without high-powered engine power.

The buzz in communities on and offline was that Red Bull had achieved marketing nirvana. This publicity event (call it a stunt, if you want) was the perfect marketing win-win. Red Bull Stratos captured the world's attention and perfectly meshed that attention with their positioning mantra of "Red Bull Gives You Wings." "I'm sure I speak for the whole Red Bull Stratos team when I say that we hoped this jump would inspire people to follow their own dreams," Baumgartner said. "I think it showed what can be accomplished with vision and teamwork—and lots of determination and persistence."

Other pundits have gone so far as to state that Red Bull Stratos may be the most successful marketing campaign of all time. Red Bull certainly broke traditional barriers of marketing to get attention for this event, skyrocketing from just another energy drink to a marketing buzz machine and making the activities of other marketing innovators look small by comparison.

The beauty of Red Bull Stratos is that it was not just a sensational stunt or event, but a business move, supported by all the company's other marketing efforts. Combined, this translated into increased sales by hundreds of millions of dollars. In the six months following the Stratos jump, sales increased by 7 percent, to $1.6 billion in the U.S., according to research firm IRI. It was the lead story in newscasts (not just sportscasts), and not a single reporter could describe the story without mentioning Red Bull. The buzz and engagement online continued, as some of the top people on Twitter—those with millions of followers—spread the word about Red Bull, the jump, the brand, and the buzz. That's value you can't put a number on.

By creating an event that was so spectacular and creative, Red Bull truly did bypass traditional marketing. "When you're in the Super Bowl, you're one of 70 ads or so. When you go around the NASCAR track, you're one of 44 teams," Ben Sturner was quoted as saying. "This is about leaving an impression . . . Every brand has an attribute that could potentially be larger than life. You need something that will transcend. In this day and age, it's about engagement and amplification of the message, and Red Bull accomplished that in both ways."

When looking at what Red Bull did with the Stratos event, here's what stands out:

! Consumer engagement
! Doing something no one else has done (Guinness World Record)
! The use of social media and viral messaging
! Brand recognition through logo saturation
! Speaking to the brand's target marketing in a big way
! Making the message and event accessible (through paid media, TV, and social media)

Step back, let your imagination loose, and test its limits. That's what will make your brand exciting. That's what will engage customers and prospects and make your brand followers more loyal. Grab their attention and go get noticed—even if it involves a jump of some kind!

MARKETING TRUTH

Taking big risks gets attention.

SHOCKING
O'DONOVAN'S IRISH PUB

Drive by North 1st Avenue in Minneapolis, Minnesota, and you're sure to notice O'Donovan's Irish Pub. Why am I so sure that you'll take notice? It's all a matter of reading between the lines—or in the case of this pub, perhaps *not* reading between the lines. Here's what I mean: O'Donovan's Irish Pub put up a huge billboard message, six stories tall, on the outside of their hardware-shop-turned-Irish-pub. The ad's message got lots of laughs and increased the patronage at this local watering hole. What was the key to such an impactful message? Some words in the message were bigger and bolder than others. So when you read the message at first glance, it read: "Naked Waitresses Flirt with You." That would get your attention, right? But if you read all the print—small and large—you'd see that it really said: "The NAKED truth about our WAITRESSES is that they only FLIRT WITH YOU to get a better tip."

Now you see what turned so many heads. This was a lesson of reading between the lines as well as a reminder that "big and bold" gets attention. (And what does it say about the target market of an Irish pub? I'll let you judge that.) In the world of marketing we always say, "Put your message where your target market is." In this case, O'Donovan's lets you read what you want to read; you then figure out that the "real" story is between the lines.

Big and bold gets attention, but it's worth mentioning as a side note that the owners also always promote the fact that they're open 365 days a year, from 3 P.M. to 2 A.M.—another eye-catcher, especially for their target market. Call it the creativity of the pub's advertising agency or guerrilla marketing, but O'Donovan's has clearly used an unconventional way of promotion that relies on imagination and words rather than big spending on print ads that may or may not hit their target market. This type of messaging is unexpected and in an unexpected place that gets talked about.

MARKETING TRUTH

Reading between the lines of big and bold can get the attention of your target market.

SHOCK AND SURPRISE: COFFEE SHOP TELEKINESIS

In a city like New York, not much shocks and surprises the natives. Shock was used, though, to attract attention for the release of the remake of the movie of Stephen King's 1974 classic horror tale, *Carrie*. As you may remember, Carrie, a high school girl, is sheltered by her deeply religious mother and unleashes a telekinetic terror on her small town after being pushed too far at her senior prom. To promote the remake, 'sNice Café in

New York's West Village was rigged to show Carrie's telekinetic powers, much to the shock of coffee shop patrons. In the video of this elaborate stunt, which went viral when released, you can see all the preparation—the construction of fake walls, a stuntman hooking a cable that would carry him up the wall, moveable tables and chairs ready to separate by the push of a remote control button, books rigged to fly off the shelf; the entire coffee shop was ready to shock and surprise.

It was business as usual in the cafe until a customer (an actor) knocks a cup of coffee onto a female patron (also an actor), drenching her papers and computer keyboard. Real customers are flabbergasted at the reaction of the young woman to the spill: Angry screams erupt and ear-splitting shouting spews forth as the young woman goes ballistic. At the peak of the fit, the unfathomable happens. The woman becomes so enraged that she uses her "telekinetic powers" to throw the man against and up the brick wall, all with a wave of her hand. The remote-controlled tables and chairs spread out on her telekinetic command, she screams, and books fly off the shelf and framed photos leap from the wall and hit the floor during her fit—all with the power of her mind. Other actors pretended to be shocked customers.

Obviously the coffee shop patrons thought they had just witnessed the unthinkable. That's exactly what the pranksters wanted: The stunt had to get noticed. And it did. The Carrie stunt got remembered and, by virtue of YouTube views, people talked about it. It became a marketing campaign that defined shock and awe; the video accumulated 4 million views overnight, eventually passing 20 million views. A hidden camera caught the customers' reactions as they stared in horror and disbelief and fled from the spooked coffee shop. It was a very effective advertising campaign that got noticed, got talked about, and got remembered—and boosted awareness of the *Carrie* remake.

So why does surprise work? Dr. Read Montague, an associate professor of neuroscience at Baylor University, suggests that people are designed to crave the unexpected. Surprise also changes behavior. When your mind is stimulated by surprise you have to immediately decide whether your beliefs or behavior need to change. The shift in behavior at the 'sNice Coffee Shop was that the patrons had to decide whether

Chapter 4 / Wild, Wacky, and Bold: Using Humor to Get Noticed

telekinesis was real or not. As this relates to marketing, we often focus on our message, what we need to say. Instead, in this case the focus should be on customer and prospect expectations. Coming at them with something unexpected produces the necessary stimulus to get noticed, talked about, and remembered.

Marketers the world over should push their brands to be more surprising. It's not something you can pull off the shelf. It's a matter of unleashing your imagination with a little courage mixed in along the way. Sometimes surprise takes guts to pull off. Try it.

MARKETING TRUTH

Marketers the world over should push their brands to be more surprising.

SURPRISE MARKETING

Your job as a marketer is to interrupt the norm, to cause the unexpected, and to shock—to surprise your target audience—all in an effort to get noticed first. When you surprise someone they will do a double-take, re-read, question, or react in some way to whatever is surprising them. Surprise creates a reaction.

If you want people to talk about you, your product, your service, your people, or your business, you have to give them something to talk about. Surprise implies that there is something new to talk about, versus what's normal and expected. In order to stimulate surprise and conversation, however, you have to understand your target market and their routine lives. Once you understand both, your marketing assignment is to disrupt, interrupt, and give them something unexpected. That's why you see crazy headlines, nutty stunts, and over-the-top events; they are very often effective marketing tools. Surprise marketing is all about creating experiences, events, and messages that people will want to share with their associates, family, and friends.

I was surprised recently when a local restaurant replied to my Foursquare check-in post. I first visited a relatively new Thai and Vietnamese restaurant in Appleton, Wisconsin, called Basil's Café. Instead of my meal being delivered by my waiter, the owner of the café stepped out and presented my lunch. My reaction: "Beauteous!" Sure, it's a contrived word of exclamation. But the owner responded by saying, "I love that word; I've never heard it before. Thanks for the compliment."

Upon returning to my office and checking my Twitter stream, the owner had replied to the check-in tweet that's automatically generated by Foursquare and simply wrote "Beauteous" in response to my check-in. I was totally surprised. I responded to his comment, retweeted it, and I'll definitely be going back to Basil's Café, not only to dine again but to connect with the owner in person. He caught me off guard with that simple one-word retweet. He also used surprise to his benefit, because he shared something and then I did, so it spread. Others saw it, commented on it, and took notice. I'm sure he got more business from others who wanted the same "beauteous" experience. It's a simple example, but it shows how the element of surprise can work.

As with any marketing message, you need to consider what emotion you want to generate as a result of the surprise. In the case of Basil's Café, they wanted me to experience and share joy. Sometimes surprise can produce excitement, shock, a double-take, or some other action on the part of the person being surprised. Regardless of the emotion it generates, surprise is very often a good way to generate word-of-mouth, helping to ensure your brand will get talked about. As a relatively new business, that's the best marketing that could happen for Basil's Café.

When I think of something showing up when least expected, one of the things that comes to mind is the Goodyear blimp. Goodyear has had a long history of using blimps to market the company. The company originally planned to use the first blimps as a way to advertise the Goodyear brand as well as renting them out to travelers. The rental plan was soon abandoned and today the blimp is only used for marketing and advertising. Whether it is on national TV or spotted overhead while attending a sporting event, the blimp gets noticed.

Chapter 4 / Wild, Wacky, and Bold: Using Humor to Get Noticed

The total cost of operating a blimp for a year is around $5 million. The blimp always makes an appearance at the Super Bowl, and the cost of a 30-second Super Bowl TV ad at the time of this writing was $4.5 million for 30 seconds. Compare this to the annual cost of operating the blimp and how many times during a Super Bowl game the blimp gets mentioned and shown. It is far more than once, making this form of marketing very cost-effective and a great branding tool the rest of the year to boot. What I like about the blimp is that it interrupts the norm; blimps aren't flying around us every day. Goodyear shows up where you don't expect it—and when they show up, you talk about it.

Goodyear estimates that more than 60 million Americans see the blimps firsthand every year, and many millions more see them on TV. Ask anyone who has seen one and they can often recall exactly when and where they saw it. That kind of recall and related word-of-mouth equity is priceless, a true marketing home run. Goodyear succeeds simply by showing up where you least expect them.

"It's been known for a long time that it's unexpected events, in particular, that drive learning," says Wael Asaad, assistant professor of neurosurgery at Brown University. Marketing strategies can be planned, developed, and executed according to a desired behavior you want from your target market. The typical thinking is simply asking the question, "What do we need to say in our ad and with our marketing messages?" The surprise approach, though, is focusing on the question, "What expectations do our customers and prospects have and how can we deliver something different to elicit a different action or reaction?"

MARKETING TRUTH

Marketers can learn from and use the element of surprise to create more effective marketing messaging and campaigns.

BEYONCÉ: MARKETING WITH NO MARKETING

This is a story about how the greatest marketing plan involved no market-ing at all. In this case, surprise was used to get noticed and the buzz that followed was not only immediate, it was a marketing eruption that was virtually unprecedented. This is the case of surprise marketing actually involving no marketing at all.

Let me explain: In the music world, album releases are a big deal. There is radio, advance sneak singles, talk show appearances, social media, and more. Pop icon Beyoncé decided to do an album release on her own terms, ignoring standard protocol. Beyoncé did the opposite of protocol, in fact, and it caught people by surprise and got noticed. Normal protocol for an album release involves a sneak single release during a major media appearance, like the Super Bowl halftime show or a commercial event like those that Pepsi hosts. Releases often happen during these mega events so as to gain maximum exposure with the buying public. Beyoncé did the Super Bowl halftime show, but she didn't release an album. Beyoncé worked with Pepsi on events and TV commercials, but she still didn't release any music. Her fan base and music pundits concluded that her next album release wasn't in the immediate future. Just when everyone was thinking that, Beyoncé dropped her new release: a complete album with a collection of companion videos, exclusively available on iTunes. The move was unprecedented.

Traditionally, new albums are released on Tuesdays. This usually happens, as I say, with the release of a teaser single for radio broadcast and distribution. Beyoncé released a *complete* album, nothing resembling a single, and not on a Tuesday. Music videos are usually made to promote singles. Beyoncé ignored this standard and filmed a video for each track, offering a full collection of videos for the album, thus creating her own standard. Usually at the time of a release, social media takes over the buzz and print media goes into action. That didn't happen either, until after the bombshell release. Many album releases are leaked during the manufacturing and distribution of CDs and DVDs. Beyoncé was able to keep her plan secret by releasing her album exclusively to iTunes. Beyoncé flipped the music industry on its head with this marketing surprise.

Beyoncé clearly wanted her music released her way, but the surprise of releasing it with no marketing is the biggest marketing ploy ever. Her explanation: "I miss that immersive experience. Now people only listen to a few seconds of songs on their iPods and they don't really invest in the whole experience. It's all about the single, and the hype. There's so much that gets between the music and the art and the fans. I felt like, I don't want anybody to get the message when my record is coming out. I just want this to come out when it's ready and from me to my fans."

Marketing should be bold and daring. Surprise works. Beyoncé went beyond bold and daring and gave a whole new definition to surprise marketing. The news of the uncharacteristic album release went viral and spread like wildfire across Twitter and Instagram once the surprise was sprung. Simply *talking about* the surprise release became the primary marketing message. Beyoncé's "marketing" move stunned the music world in an unheard-of fashion, ignoring the normal marketing machine of singles, performances, interviews, and appearances. Call it shock or surprise; Beyoncé can call it success.

The message here is that even if you aren't Beyoncé, you can still surprise your market just by going against the norm. That's what people will talk about as much as what you are marketing.

MARKETING TRUTH

Marketing should be bold and daring, and the element of surprise works.

CONTROVERSY
GoDaddy.com

Shock and controversy can go hand-in-hand. The website developer and domain supplier GoDaddy.com loves to create controversy with shock, so we have both covered here. The first thing any good TV commercial must do is to capture the viewer's attention. It could be with something funny, shocking, or even gross; GoDaddy.com has touched on all three in their mission to get your attention.

Let's go right to controversial topic number one: grossness. A recent GoDaddy.com ad starred supermodel Bar Refaeli paired up with a geeky love interest. The two were shown in an extremely close-up kiss. It was the Super Bowl ad you couldn't look away from: a supermodel and a nerd making out. Known as the "Perfect Match" commercial, the supermodel kissed Walter, the computer programmer, visually portraying the "smart meets sexy" mantra of GoDaddy.com. As with any Super Bowl marketing, the question is always, "Is it worth it?" or "Does it work?" People definitely talked about this ad, and ginning up some controversy (by grossing out viewers) helped this Super Bowl commercial generate buzz and accomplished the advertiser's business goals. After this particular Super Bowl GoDaddy called its ad campaign a "sensational Super Bowl victory," and company CEO Blake Irving said the company set "all-time Super Bowl Sunday records" for mobile sales, website hosting, and new customers.

The company did acknowledge, though, that the ad created two factions: supporters and non-supporters, who called the ad inappropriate. Even so, it attracted more than four million YouTube views even before it aired during the Super Bowl. Controversy got attention. GoDaddy.com stated that the goal of this Super Bowl ad was to be memorable and create buzz. In doing so, they used humor to demonstrate an edgy side and technical smarts. That kiss generated a lot of attention and in the process "polarized viewers," said Irving. "Many, including me, thought it was awkward and funny, and a few thought it was over the top." In this case, *all* of those characterizations worked in getting attention. On the Tuesday following that Super Bowl the company reported its biggest sales day in company history and shared the following stats to illustrate the increases it saw over the comparable day the year before:

- ❗ Hosting sales jumped 45 percent
- ❗ Dotcom domain sales rose 40 percent
- ❗ New mobile customers increased by 35 percent
- ❗ 10,000 new customers

Specifically, the "Perfect Match" commercial had two goals: 1) Get the attention of potential customers; and 2) hammer the product and brand name into potential customers' minds. Widespread hatred and controversy over the ad are clear indicators that they are, if nothing else, attention-getting.

The commercial was helped with a unique execution that had a simple premise: smart meets sexy. GoDaddy.com is a seamless, smooth combination of the two forces. Bar Refaeli represents the sexy element, while actor Jesse Heiman symbolizes the nerdy, smart element. Combine the two traits and you have GoDaddy; combine the two characters and you have the kiss that grosses viewers out, makes them uncomfortable, and makes an indelible impression. The last is a marketing home run.

Marketers often try to do what GoDaddy.com did in the commercial: Lure customers with a sexy offer and keep them with smart products/ services/support, all while making a positive, long-lasting impression. Any marketing that does this works.

MARKETING TRUTH

Focusing on a smart, original, innovative message that is backed up by effective content will sell products, even if the message is controversial.

TACO BELL

This story is relevant to our discussion of how to use controversy effectively in your marketing, but we've put it here because it's an oldie but goodie. In case you haven't noticed, one of the best marketing companies out there is Taco Bell. They try the extreme, out-of-the-box ideas that definitely get noticed. But before we get to Taco Bell's use of controversy to get noticed, let's look at one more thing the company did to get noticed: In 2001, there was a Russian spaceship called Mir circling the earth. As you might know, when spaceships return to earth they need to eject the cosmonauts/ astronauts after re-entry into the earth's atmosphere, more or less blowing up the remaining spaceship or letting it fall to earth. Taco Bell found out about this and had a 40-by-40-foot tarpaulin painted with a Taco Bell logo as the target in the middle of that tarp. They took it off the coast of Australia and threw it in the Pacific Ocean and announced to the media that if any part of the Mir spaceship fell and hit their target, everyone in America would receive a free taco. Their marketing tactic got noticed. Everyone was talking about it as the spaceship prepared its landing. In the end, the spaceship landed 10 miles off the coast of Chile, so Taco Bell was safe. For the price of a tarpaulin with a corporate bull's-eye Taco Bell gained market share in the fast-food category, something very challenging to achieve today.

Now, on to their controversial action.

It was April Fools' Day, 1996. Back then, Taco Bell used newspaper advertising. The ads featured the Liberty Bell in Philadelphia. On April Fools' Day, Taco Bell claimed in the ads that they'd bought the iconic symbol and renamed it the "Taco Liberty Bell." There were complaints, but there were also media hits. There was controversy; the stunt definitely got noticed. Taco Bell finally ended up explaining the joke. Consumers, although drowned in controversy at the time, relented and many liked the brand even more. Taco Bell took a risk with a controversial tactic, but it paid off with plenty of marketing buzz. Sometimes controversy pays—but it's important to be careful.

Well, that was risk and controversy. Now I will ask you, which is better: an aha! moment or the WOW factor? I'll let you decide and prepare to be "Wow-ed" in the next chapter.

MARKETING TRUTH

Using controversy as a tactic in your marketing can be risky, but it can also be very successful.

THE
WOW
FACTOR

W ITH 245 HOTELS REPRESENTING UPWARDS OF 70,000 ROOMS, New York City is dense with hotels. So standing out among all 245 is not always easy. Getting noticed is a real marketing challenge. The Algonquin Hotel figured out a way to do it, though. The Algonquin Hotel is on what is known as "Club Row" in midtown Manhattan. The significance of this is that this hotel was once the site of the Algonquin Roundtable, a gathering place of elite, sophisticated spirit-sippers of the 1930s. That historical ambience inspired the Algonquin Hotel to create something that would make them stand out. The Algonquin Hotel created a featured drink known as "Martini on the Rock." This was no ordinary drink, mind you. This was no ordinarily *priced* drink, either. The price tag to imbibe this cocktail is a mere $10,000. That certainly garners attention, but the Algonquin wanted positive attention. Problem solved. The "Martini on the Rock" comes with a diamond sparkling on the bottom of the drink. (The drink requires 72-hour advance notice and a personal visit to the hotel's own jeweler.) Hotel marketers promoted the fact that it's the best way to arrange a marriage proposal, complete with a drink that will live up to the special moment.

LUXURY GETS NOTICED

Besides being diamond-adorned, the drink itself is the vesper martini, another attention-getting point. The vesper martini was made popular by James Bond movies and novels. In the movies it is the martini associated with the phrase "shaken, not stirred." In the novels, the vesper martini, the spy's drink of choice, was vodka with a hint of gin and a French aperitif called Lillet. At the bottom of the Algonquin's vesper martini is a diamond exceeding 1.5 carats. The cut is known as "radiant," which offers more than the usual sparkle, especially when covered in vodka.

The idea was picked up subsequent to the Algonquin Hotel's creation by the Ritz Carlton Tokyo. The Ritz's drink, named "Diamonds Are Forever," was priced at $22,000 and referred to as the Ritz's Diamond Martini. Take that, Algonquin Hotel. To draw attention to the hotel's grand opening, the Ritz took Grey Goose vodka and a hint of lime, plus the special garnish of a one-carat diamond, then stirred or shook the drink over ice and poured it into a traditional martini glass. Four martinis were reportedly sold, but the value of the publicity far outweighed the profits or losses on the drink itself. (One purchase was for a marriage proposal and the other three occasions were anniversary celebrations.)

Across the country and world, swanky bars continue to vie to serve the costliest cocktail. Here are a couple of more contenders, as reported by CNN:

! *World Cocktail.* A blend of grape juice, lemon juice, simple syrup, 23-karat edible liquid gold, Pineau des Charentes, and bitters, topped with Veuve Clicquot champagne. Served at Trump Tower in New York City.

❗ *The Benjamin Margarita.* Three exquisite, extra *añejo* (or "ultra-aged") tequilas go into this cocktail, named after the $100 bill (which is also the price of the drink): Patron Burdelos, Herradura Selection Suprema, and Partida Elegante, some Grand Marnier Cuvee du Cent Cinquentenaire, 100 percent organic agave syrup, fresh lime juice, and Louis XIII cognac, with a garnish of blood orange caviar and edible-gold-and-kosher-salt rim. Served by Red O Restaurant in Los Angeles.

These flashy cocktails get noticed, but more than that, they get talked about. These places become known for their drinks. One of the goals of getting noticed is becoming known. Becoming known continually gets talked about. I'm sure you'll drink to that.

If something is ridiculously expensive, does it always get noticed? That's probably what Starbucks was hoping when the company came out with a $450, all-metal gift card for the 2013 holiday season. According to the description, each card is "hand-assembled, features a gorgeous artisan rose base metal and rose-colored coating." Only 1,000 cards were available during the holiday period. The cards went on sale at a partner's website and sold out almost instantly, in six minutes. It has been reported that one in 10 adults in the U.S. received a Starbucks gift card as a gift item in 2012, making a Starbucks card one of the most gifted items in the United States.

MARKETING TRUTH

Luxury items with limited availability can create enough demand to cause tremendous marketing buzz.

THREE-DIMENSIONAL MAIL

Direct mail is *not* dead. Direct marketing is alive and well, in fact, especially with all that you can do with personalized URLs (personalized website addresses). We won't cover personalized URLs in this book, but I recommend you learn about them. We will cover, however, how much attention you can get from three-dimensional mail, also known as "lumpy mail." What happens when you get something in the mail that's lumpy? You want to open it to find out what is causing the lumps, right? Getting opened is a huge marketing goal when it comes to direct mail.

3D Mail Results, a division of American Retail Supply, supplies 3D mail products, premiums, and promotional products for all your lumpy direct-mail needs. A review of their product listing shows a great array of lumpy mail examples that get attention every day. Take note of the imagination at work here and think about how you can adapt these to your messages so you get noticed. Here are just a few:

- ! A real boomerang for a "We want you back!" campaign
- ! A round wooden half-dollar-sized chip with the word TUIT printed on it, along with, "You keep saying you will call us when you get around to it ('a round TUIT'). Now you have no excuse."
- ! A self-mailing message in a real bottle
- ! An imprinted bank bag that's used for deposits
- ! A toy compass: "Are you lost?"
- ! A large plastic insect: "This is the last time I'm going to bug you"
- ! Plastic scissors for any message related to cutting costs

The ideas for three-dimensional mail are only limited by your imagination. I once increased cash flow by putting candy mints into the invoice envelope that got delivered to the accounting department of my customers. Accounting people like attention too! Lumpy mail did the trick in this case.

Coconut Greetings, an Ohio company specializing in painted coconut greetings, invitations, and promotional incentives, found that coconuts can be mailed without a box or package. One of their clients was a country music TV station that sent 800 coconuts to DJs around the country, promoting a new reality series that happened to be filmed in Hawaii. The coconuts were a natural association, and they were noticed and kept. (Nobody throws coconuts away.) You can bet the coconuts were talked about, too, when people asked why there was a decorative coconut on the recipient's desk.

Why does lumpy mail work? One reason is that your direct mail can't be successful unless it gets opened. Another reason is that people are bored with traditional marketing and advertising. 3D mail is entertaining and engages the prospect or customer. Engaged customers take an interest, stay involved with your message, and take action as a result.

> ## MARKETING TRUTH
>
> *Direct mail is not dead.*

CUTE PUPPIES

There's no doubt that "cute" gets noticed. And nothing epitomizes the cute category more than puppies. So why do cute puppies have the effect that they do on us? Psychological researchers have found that certain features in baby animals trigger an affectionate response within the brain. Baby animals—with their round faces, bright, deep-set eyes, big cheeks, furry limbs, and carefree nature—are cute to humans. One reason is that our own babies have similar characteristics. Our parenting instincts are also stimulated by these traits. Even if you're not a mother or father, these traits stimulate our natural nurturing instincts. These instincts are related to survival and anything related to babies stimulate these instincts.

Another factor at work here is the feeling of pleasure that cute things bring. Newer psychological studies show that cute is an immediate stimulant in boosting our brain's pleasure neurons. That's why, of course, cute animals are constantly used in marketing to encourage consumers to buy products or take action, because of these pleasurable and nurturing qualities.

On a recent trip to Rome, I noticed that most of the homeless people I saw seeking donations on the streets had a cute animal by their side, usually a dog. I've seen homeless people on the streets of Chicago, New York, and other big cities, but rarely accompanied by a furry mate. A French university found that the homeless are given larger donations more frequently if a puppy accompanies them. Studies from the same university also found that women are more likely to notice and eventually date a man if a puppy is with him. Laugh if you want, but cute gets noticed.

Researchers have also found that babies that are deemed cute triggered a mechanism over and above normal parenting that made parents more willing and happier to drop other things to care for the child. Simply put, we focus on cute. Whether it's big eyes, a sweet smile, a wagging tale, or a sad look, we take notice and want to care and help. Wanting to care for something that can't care for itself and the sense that something so cute can't be dangerous also contribute to the likability that cute things encourage in us, and what makes them so effective in marketing messaging.

From a marketing point of view, cuteness is also understood across many cultures, making it the perfect tool, especially in international markets; just look at the cute factor that the Japanese use in marketing Pokémon and Hello Kitty. In the English-speaking world, and primarily in America, this is exemplified by Elmo, Furby, and Mickey Mouse. Cuteness was certainly used to gain attention in the old Shirley Temple movies. More recently, the 2006 animated movie *Happy Feet* featured cuteness as a marketing tool. What's not cute about a cartoon penguin, after all?

Stephen Jay Gould, an evolutionary biologist and science historian, remarked on the phenomenon of cute in the journal *Natural History*, in which he pointed out that "over time Mickey Mouse had been drawn more and more to resemble an infant—with a bigger head, bigger eyes, and so forth." Gould suggested that this change in Mickey's image was intended to increase his popularity by making him appear cuter. Researchers at Cleveland State University have published their findings on what they called "the roots of 'cute' and its evolution with reference to its relevance to marketers." Marketers are always looking to better understand any link between social loyalty and consumer consumption. In the case of

---

MARKETING TRUTH

Cuteness and niceness are understood across many cultures, making them the perfect marketing tools in international markets.

---

the Cleveland State University research, one area of concentration was understanding the contribution of "cuteness" marketing.

Examples of cute items cited in the study, published in the *Journal of Consumer Culture*, included Victoria's Secret's Pink label; Day-Glo accessories and retro sneakers linked to 1980s rave culture; and cars such as the Mini Cooper and Volkswagen. The cuteness factor contributed to these products' popularity and "social loyalty" and led to an increase in consumer consumption.

MOM-TO-BE: RED ROBIN

This is not a book on PR but on getting attention, getting remembered, and getting talked about. You can say that this is the job of PR, but its job is also gaining positive media attention. That's exactly what a Red Robin restaurant in Apex, North Carolina, did when its manager comp'd a very pregnant customer (she was actually overdue) when she stopped in for a meal with her husband and 2-year-old son. The manager's kind offer— which cost $11.50—garnered national media attention. On the register receipt he also generated a rough message to the expectant mother: "MOM 2 BEE GOOD LUC." The media got hold of the gesture and the message flooded national news outlets with this bit of news about a random act of kindness from a Red Robin employee.

In interviews about the comp'd expectant mother's tab, the manager stated that the way to make customers happy is to "listen to them and make sure they leave feeling appreciated and valued. If our guests know we welcome their feedback, I think they'll talk with us and speak up . . . to say they had a positive and satisfying experience with us, and hopefully also to say they'll be back again soon." According to the manager, what he did was part of the Red Robin corporate culture, which calls these "unbridled acts," a simple act of kindness. "Treating our guests in a way that's special and unlike anything they'll experience at other restaurants helps us stand apart in a world where there are many options for dining out," the manager explained. "Our goal is to create lasting memories for the individuals and families who visit our restaurants."

This is starting to sound familiar, right? Adding something extra and special is part of the "WOW Factor" formula for gaining attention and getting remembered. The get-noticed, get-remembered, get-talked-about lesson here is about showing the positive impact of a random act of kindness.

Being cute and nice happens live and in person. Nothing gets noticed like physical engagement. Can the same thing happen online? Let's take a look in the next chapter for the answer to that question.

MARKETING TRUTH

A simple act of kindness goes a long way in getting noticed and talked about.

6

GETTING NOTICED ONLINE

ONLINE MARKETERS LIKE THE COST-EFFECTIVENESS ASSOCIATED with ecommerce and marketing, but it's become a very competitive world. From an ecommerce point of view, Amazon alone has more than two million seller accounts. You may have developed the best website in the world, but if no one sees it, what good does it do you? Understanding how best to market your site—getting your site noticed—is a requirement if you want to be a successful business. To attract attention you need to apply smart marketing techniques that differentiate you from your competitors.

People come to you for something, whether it's a product, service, or information. I believe that content truly is king, so packing your website, emails, articles, and ebooks with relevant and valuable information will set you apart from websites that are simply on-line brochures. Your goal here is to become the "go-to" source for anything and everything related to your expertise.

Usually I offer advice about what you should do, but now I'm going to give you a "don't": Don't use the online gimmicks of yesterday. Internet users are fed up with pop-up ads, fly-ins, pop-up bubbles, exit pages, spam email, and other unsolicited information. Many users, in fact, have applications that block pop-up and other intrusive, annoying ads, which means you may not even be reaching a potential reader of your content.

CONTENT

In content terms, "talking up" your product, service, or brand is about using specific details, focusing on the benefits to the reader, and com-municating big ideas in a way that's always relevant and valuable to your customer or prospect. Sometimes that means just telling it like it is and not trying to do anything more. Think about your reader, customer, or prospect and make sure the content is all about them.

Building in a sense of urgency and anticipation works, especially when using content. If you have a big announcement to make, start the anticipation sequence far in advance. People generally like and respond well to anticipation. Suspenseful thrillers, murder mysteries, and "bridezilla" activity leading up to a wedding are examples of this. People like the build-up along the way.

When creating content that gets noticed, write like you speak. Write to inform. Keep the gloss, glitz, and glamour to a minimum. No one cares about the extent of your vocabulary. Make your communication more like a conversation with a friend. This is what will build trust with your reader.

MARKETING TRUTH

Smart marketing techniques that differentiate you from your competition are necessary when creating content that gets noticed.

Offer your reader value and communicate with them with information that they will find useful, valuable, and relevant. Write in short sentences in a way that everyone understands (even if a few grammar rules are broken along the way).

GETTING EMAILS NOTICED AND OPENED

Let's get right to the point: Is anyone today getting too few emails? I'm sure I'm safe in assuming that your answer is no. The trick is to figure out how the emails you send as a marketer fall into the category of those that get opened and not in the junk, spam, or otherwise useless category.

Here's what people really want in their email inbox:

! Timely information
! Reward or benefit for taking quick action
! Useful information
! Personal invitations
! Necessary information
! Fresh news that's helpful and relevant

People also immediately recognize pitchy, spam email subject lines because they tend to contain the following:

! The word *free*
! "Percent off" special offers
! Subject lines that are too long
! Pleas for help
! Too-good-to-be-true statements
! Bait-and-switch ploys
! Requests for donations
! Anything with an exclamation point

Email subject lines need to attract attention, just like headlines do. The best email subject lines are short, to the point, and provide enough information to lead the reader to want to explore your message further. Trying to stand out in someone's inbox by using splashy or cheesy phrases will invariably result in your email being ignored.

Consider the following best practices related to email marketing and getting your messages noticed (and eventually opened at a higher rate):

❗ *Plan your email delivery frequency, but make sure you're consistent, both in what you deliver and how often you send it.* If subscribers expect to hear from you every month, send them an email every month. If they expect special offers and news, send special offers and news. The goal is to engage your audience and condition them to open your emails as they get them.

❗ *Offer content that is interesting, fresh, and relevant.* This may sound like a broken record, but for all your marketing messaging this is truly the best formula for engaging your target market.

❗ *Avoid spammy subject lines.* As noted above, using words like "free" or "X percent off," or anything with an exclamation point, screams spam and junk mail to your recipient.

❗ *Send the email from you—your name—not an impersonal or vague email address.* Sending email from a no-reply address detaches you from the relationship you're trying to build with your target audience.

❗ *Keep the subject line short and sweet.* Don't use the subject line to attempt to convey all your marketing. Those that regularly read email messages typically will scan the subject line fast, only seeing the first three to five words, especially if using a smartphone or tablet to check email. This means putting the most important part of your subject line at the beginning.

❗ *The better you can communicate your story in just a few words, the more likely your email will be opened.* Think about what would make you open a particular email. On the flip side, what would make you delete an email? Understanding both of these will provide you with guidance for crafting your subject line.

❗ *Ask short questions, create a sense of urgency, be outrageous, and make people wonder.* Funny works too! People like inside information, secrets, and exclusive information. Communicate those characteristics as appropriate.

! *Write one-to-one.* Craft your emails as if you were talking to a friend. Keep your messages conversational and as if it's just you and your recipient communicating. Those receiving your message want to feel like you're talking directly to them, not the masses. They want to feel like they're the only one that received the email you sent. Whatever you do, avoid sounding like you are reading from a call center telemarketing script.

! *Send emails when you think your receiver will open them or see them.* This is hard to predict, so you may have to check your email analytics or test different days and times to see how timing affects your open rates.

! *Don't overload your emails with lots of corporate-speak or tech talk.* Conversation among friends typically doesn't contain these, so don't load up your emails any differently.

! *Keep email messages positive.* We already mentioned that your content needs to be useful, interesting, fresh, and relevant. Information crafted in this way will also lend itself to creating the best attention-getting subject lines.

! *Don't over-communicate.* Only send an email when you have something valuable or helpful for your targets. Your recipient will be looking for benefits that make them smarter, feel better, and save them time and money. Write accordingly.

! *Use words that are emotional or are sensory.* These attract attention and help your subject lines stand out in crowded inboxes.

Build relationships with your email list. Consistency and relevance will help recipients learn to expect your emails. The techniques listed here and the recognition of your name in the email's "from" field will increase your email open rate.

MARKETING TRUTH

Email subject lines need to attract attention, just like headlines do.

THE MARKETING HOOK

Some of the best marketing uses a marketing "hook" to get heard above the flood of information threatening to drown audiences. One definition of a marketing hook is a short phrase, word, or jingle that entices a customer to do something. Another definition, and the way we use it in *Market Like You Mean It*, is: information designed to arouse interest in a product, service, or company and that spurs interaction between the prospect and the product, service, or company.

One of the best marketing hooks is information. The world of information overload we're all dealing with can also be viewed as a world of information availability. People who shop seek information first. People who buy seek more information. Information can be a differentiator, but most of all it can be an attention-getter. Take a look at any traditional advertisement, a Yellow Pages ad (remember those?), or any display advertisement. Most, in my opinion, look pretty much the same and are lost or diluted among all the messages and are rendered ineffective. Imagine one ad in that cesspool, however, that offers a top-10 list, a free special article, or a DVD to get more information about the product, service, or company. Which one will generate action and engagement? The one offering information as a hook.

Simply put, valuable and interesting information will be read. Information can be used, in the form of a hook, to move prospects into the paying-customer category. The information you offer doesn't have to be elaborate, but it does have to be interesting and valuable to your customer or prospect. Imagine, for example, an article from a financial planner called "Seven Mistakes People Make When Hiring a Financial Planner." If you're in the market for a financial planner you will want to see that article, so you may request a copy and even be motivated to make contact with the person offering that information. They have hooked you into their "funnel" with something valuable, in this case, information.

An ideal place to use your marketing hook to get noticed is on your own website. Imagine a prospect landing on your page and spotting in a starburst an offer for a free report or a special article. If you're in the productivity business, your report might be titled "Make Twice as Much Money and Take One More Day Off a Week." Would that get your attention?

It would get mine; who doesn't want more money and more time off? The website visitor landing on that page sees that hook and clicks accordingly, even though they may not know you or know if you are likable or trustworthy. Your visitor clicks the offer in the starburst graphic, registers on your site with their email address to get the report, and the report is immediately emailed to them. Within seconds, the report arrives and is read by your now-engaged website visitor, who has a reason to like you and trust you—the start of a potentially valuable relationship. After the initial report is delivered, the visitor receives more information and another marketing hook—this time perhaps it's a webinar, ebook, or PDF download. Welcome to the world of content marketing.

It is at this point that you have turned an unsuspecting prospect into a potentially satisfied client, referral source, and brand advocate, all with the exchange of a little bit of information, all starting with your marketing hook. In this case, the marketing goal is to find people interested in what you have to say and eventually get them interested in what you sell. By offering a sample of your value, you start the process of turning a prospect into a paying customer. Getting noticed started this process. Getting remembered furthered the process along a nurturing path. And getting talked about is the outcome that grows your business.

MARKETING TRUTH

A marketing hook is information designed to arouse interest in a product, service, or company and that spurs interaction between the prospect and the product, service, or company.

GETTING NOTICED IN SOCIAL MEDIA COMMUNITIES

When you last visited the Twittersphere, how many people were talking at the same time as you were? You may not have known it, but there were literally millions of screaming "voices," all trying to be heard. How then do you get noticed, followed, and heard to make your social media marketing efforts worth your while? First, ignore the fact that millions are talking when you are. You don't need conversations with all of them; you don't *want* a conversation with all of them. You don't need millions of prospects in order to be successful. You only need a qualified few.

It doesn't matter how many Facebook friends you have or how many Twitter followers you have. You don't need your blog viewed daily by thousands of people. All you need is to get in front of those that can and want to buy from you. All you need is to get in front of key influencers in your community or market. In marketing there is an age-old, fundamental question: "Does everyone that can buy from you know about you?" This same fundamental question applies to the sea of social media swimmers. That is very good news. You can now concentrate on adding real value to the small group that matters most. This gives you time to contribute, collaborate, and engage in more meaningful conversations and start to build essential relationships within your community or market.

Social media has become a pool of hashtags. Hashtags (which use the pound sign, #) allow Twitter and Facebook users to tag tweets to give more context to the content they're sharing and to index content and conversations. Hashtags can also be used as a way to track a status update or tweet or share to a particular conversation or chat. On TV, many commentators and hosts use hashtags as a way to get viewers to ask questions (for example, #asktheexpert). Hashtags get noticed and remembered, especially when you want to come back to conversations outside of real time.

Here are some guidelines about how to use social media marketing to your advantage:

! *Be attractive and welcoming.* Imagine your social networks as the living room of your home. You want your followers to be your guests. You want them to feel comfortable with the conversation. You want to be interesting, fresh, and relevant to stay engaged with them. You are being watched closely in this situation. Act the same way in the online community environment and your authenticity will shine through and win out.

! *Be friendly and chatty.* You can't bore people into buying or into relationships. Usually the noisy, conversational, and opinionated participants in social communities create more followers and more relationships. Quiet is less noticeable. Bold and outgoing get attention. In social media, strong talkers and silent lurkers don't partner well. Ask questions, conduct polls, inform, entertain, and inspire your followers, and talk about trending topics. That's how to stick out in your communities without worrying about the millions outside of your circles.

! *Be interesting.* Being conversational and chatty is not always enough. Make sure that your discussions are interesting. Don't be boring, but be true to your mission and brand and stay real in your conversation. Show others you care about them. Be thought-provoking. Create a "wow factor" with fresh and relevant content.

Standing out in social media communities simply boils down to the fact that you have to be social. It's not a "build it and they will come" strategy. You can't throw up a Facebook page, open a Twitter account, and simply post sales-y content. Social implies two-way conversation, not one-way promotional messages. Social media is all about the development of relationships; people do business with people they know, like, and trust.

The online world levels the playing field for all involved. Each person's voice has an equal opportunity to be heard. It's up to you to offer something interesting and relevant that others want to hear. Do that and you will get noticed, remembered, and talked about.

Whether it's an old-fashioned quilting circle, a gathering at the corner store, or attending a cocktail party, people inherently want to share and discuss information about their lives, friends, news, ideas, and so on. Doing this with the help of technology and a multimedia mix of words, pictures, video, and audio is what social media marketing is all about. To be successful in any community—whether social media or traditional—human nature must be understood. That means understanding what captures your community members' attention, what keeps them engaged, and what makes them want to share. If you want to get noticed, pay attention to what captures the imagination, hearts, souls, and minds of your friends, connections, and followers.

Every community is unique, but in general, the things that appeal to community members and help you stand out in the social media tsunami are the same:

! *Shock and awe.* Morbid and extreme photos get noticed and are shared quickly.

! *Emotion.* Videos that bring a tear to our eye get commented on and shared. Watch any video of a service member's surprise reunion with his or her family and I guarantee you will need a tissue.

! *Funny.* Random, crazy stunts or events that make us laugh spread like wildfire in social communities.

! *Motivational.* Words of encouragement, inspirational quotes, success stories, and other upbeat communication get noticed. Once again, sharing happens because you want others to feel what you felt when reading these types of posts.

! *New and fresh.* Whether a new idea, a refinement to something you already know, an experience you wished for that someone else had, we all crave new and fresh information and love to share it.

! *Interesting.* People obviously gravitate toward things they are interested in.

! *Targeted messaging.* You have to know who you want to talk to and what communities they're involved in. This translates into understanding your audience better and why you want someone's attention.

! *Consistency.* Maintain a social presence and don't get known by your absence. Once you start, keep it up. Engage. Discuss. Ask questions. Challenge viewpoints. Talk with people, not at them. Just be consistent in your approach and the frequency with which you post and engage with your community on social media.

MARKETING TRUTH

Be fresh, relevant, and interesting. Share and engage with fellow community members. Create and facilitate two-way conversations. Respond and converse consistently. Show others that you care about them.

! *Dialog.* Always remember that it's a two-way conversation. That means talking and listening. (Most forget about the listening part.) If you don't listen well, you will get ejected out of communities quickly. Find conversations going on about your company, your products, or your services and jump in. Listen first, then converse.

You want to get noticed in online communities using social media marketing? Be fresh, relevant, and interesting. Share and engage with fellow community members. Create and facilitate two-way conversations. Respond and converse consistently. Show others that you care about them. Do these things and you will bust through marketing clutter, on- and offline.

HOW TO MAKE YOUR CONTENT MARKETING STAND OUT

Marketing has had a great journey, starting from the day the wheel was invented and its inventor needed someone to buy it, until today. We have passed through the days of "the four Ps" (price, place, product, and promotion), traditional marketing, guerrilla marketing, and strategic marketing. In the past five to eight years (light years, in internet time!), we've skipped along a path of social media marketing. An important stone on the path is content marketing.

Lead generation (finding prospective customers) for today's companies is driven by inbound marketing, which is driven by content marketing. This is the most efficient, least expensive method of lead generation, especially for B2B ("business to business") companies. This type of lead generation is also known as inbound marketing.

As a point of reference, let me define these marketing components: Lead generation is the generation of a customer or prospect's interest or inquiry into a product or service. Inbound marketing is marketing a company through social media and content vehicles such as blogs, ebooks, and enewsletters that serve to earn the attention of customers and prospects to the brand, product, service, or company. This is in contrast to direct marketing, direct sales, advertising, and other "outbound marketing."

Content marketing is any marketing that involves the creation, distribution, and sharing of relevant and interesting media and publishing content in order to attract, acquire, and engage customers and prospects, while motivating them to take further action.

Now, consider that anything and everything can be found online. More consumers are looking to educate themselves before buying, and it is through your content that they learn. Those companies that do the best job educating consumers are often the ones that win the business. Trust with customers and prospects is developed by educating and informing them. Very often, the most trusted company is the one that a consumer buys from.

Building this trust, however, takes time and a lot of information (content). The challenge for you as a marketer is often managing your time and resources while producing a steady flow of content. This is where having a content marketing strategy comes in.

First, buyers and prospects have to find your content. When they find it, it's because they have become aware of a particular challenge and are evaluating available options for a product or service that will solve their problem. If your content isn't easy to find, doesn't get noticed, or doesn't provide the answers they're seeking, the buyers will move on to a different provider who is more helpful. So you want your content marketing to stand out, especially as more marketers use this form of marketing to connect with prospects and customers.

There is no doubt that content marketing has grown exponentially in recent years. Every time you turn around, there's a new thought leader offering a new perspective, a new level of expertise, and more information to help buyers make decisions. Here are some strategies to get noticed, remembered, and talked about in your content marketing:

! *Content ideas.* Ideas are the specific content points that you want to communicate and that you believe people are seeking. Ideas are also the stories, examples, and case studies that connect with your prospects. Good content ideas showcase your expertise and are the foundation of your content marketing plan.

! *How-tos.* Take an idea a step further and tell your readers how to use the information; this will get you noticed. These are solutions that solve a problem or otherwise meet your customer's challenges.

Offering a continuous flow of "how-to" content will endear you to your prospects.

! *The content plan.* At a minimum you want to plan out who you're talking to, what you want to say to your audience, how often you will communicate, and with what vehicle(s). These are the same principles as with any aspect of marketing but they are especially essential with content marketing.

! *Online marketing.* This is mostly known as search engine optimization (SEO). SEO has the ability to put your content right in front of your prospects' eyeballs when they're doing an online search, so you'll be found when someone is looking for what you're offering. The better you can optimize your content so that it always shows up at the top, or near the top, of search results, the more the content will get noticed and consumed.

! *Social media marketing.* The other key to getting your content marketing noticed is the distribution of the content. Typically, content is distributed via websites, email, or social media marketing. Social media marketing builds and fuels the relationships that make content marketing work. Social media also fuels sharing that is essential in getting more content noticed on an ongoing basis.

Start with these tactics when developing your content marketing. They will keep you focused and help your messaging get noticed in the content storm that surrounds us every day.

By now you have noticed how to get noticed. That's the first step in effective marketing. Get prepared as we look at how to make that notoriety stick in the minds of your prospects. It's time to make that message remembered. Let's look at some ways that you can achieve that and get your target market to act in the way you want them to.

MARKETING TRUTH

To make your content stand out, become a thought leader, or offer a new perspective or level of expertise.

GET
REMEMBERED

MOTIVATING CUSTOMERS AND PROSPECTS TO TAKE ACTION

GETTING REMEMBERED IS ONE OF THE RESULTS OF EFFECTIVE marketing. As you're learning in this book, capturing the prospect or customer's attention is the first goal. Getting remembered is the second goal, on the way to talking about products, services, companies, and people—all to motivate prospects to take action. Marketing is made up of many, many things working together to make this motivation happen. Communicating in a clear and consistent matter that reflects the positioning of a company or organization contributes to this.

By now you know that much marketing is interruptive. Customers and prospects have to stop what they are doing to pay attention to your marketing. Once the interruption takes place, marketing must be memorable in order to be effective. We've talked about how 90 percent of purchasing decisions are made with the subconscious mind. The way to get to the subconscious is through the repetition of your marketing messages.

Here are some marketing truths for creating memorable marketing that will motivate your prospect to take action. This is how you market like you mean it and get remembered:

- ! Aim at your target market and talk directly to them.
- ! Reveal benefits, not just features. Features tell, benefits sell.
- ! Give your marketing a voice, look, and feel that is consistent and noticeable. Make sure it reflects who you are as a company, your positioning, values, and beliefs. Positioning is the perception of your brand in the mind of your prospect.
- ! Communicate the competitive advantage of what you offer, the benefit you offer that the competition doesn't.
- ! Make your messaging simple. Don't confuse the prospect. Simple, concise, clear messages are easier to remember.
- ! Find a memorable style and stick with it. Don't make a lot of changes as you go.
- ! Identify the action you're motivating prospects to take as a result of your marketing. In marketing these are called "calls to action." Every brochure, website, sales pitch, and more ought to have a call to action associated with it. Do not leave it to chance that customers and prospects know what to do as a result of your marketing.
- ! Communicate in a personal style. People like to do business with people they like, know, and trust. People do business with people, not logos, not icons, and not company names. Use pictures of people in all your marketing to help your messages to be remembered.
- ! Last, but not least, make sure your messages are ethical and truthful.

Let's take a look at a few of these truths in action. In 2012, Procter & Gamble launched a "Thank You, Mom" campaign featuring Olympic athletes training under the watch and influence of their mothers. P&G not only leveraged a current event, the Summer Olympic Games, they also stayed true to their brand and the audience to which they market. Media coverage of the "Thank You, Mom" campaign exploded, allowing the company to reach beyond their primary target. People remembered the commercials, print ads, and the campaign overall.

You have probably heard about Samsung going up against Apple products with its "The Next Best Thing Is Already Here" campaign. Samsung didn't mention Apple by name, but the campaign did point out every competitive advantage they had when compared to Apple products. Samsung focused on the benefits they offered that the competition didn't. They threw in a little humor and talk about the ad took off and spread. Their campaign was remembered when it came out and still is today, many months after the start of their campaign.

General Electric led B2B social media trends by using Instagram, Tumblr, Facebook, and Twitter to engage with their customers and target market. General Electric often features people in their many ads. For example, an ad might show the GE employee behind one of the company's products interacting with a customer, thereby giving a face to their target market. General Electric has a consistent, engaging message that speaks to its customers and engages followers; content might include stories about how the company has built close-knit teams, or what's going on in employees' hometowns, or corporate efforts to make communities where GE has offices more environmentally friendly. Their approach is personal, interesting, and very engaging. This bucked some B2B marketing trends at the time and set a new standard for getting remembered and talked about.

Whether selling or getting a prospect interested in what you offer, doing so online is effective. Knowing how your target market thinks will guide you in your messaging. Next, let's take a look inside the mind of your prospect.

MARKETING TRUTH

Features tell, but benefits sell.

SOCIAL
PSYCHOLOGY

W HAT MAKES YOU SHARE SOMETHING WITH SOMEONE ELSE? Usually it's something that was interesting, outrageous, hilarious, cool, or unusual, or perhaps it was an idea that helped you in some way, saved you money, or saved you time.

THE PSYCHOLOGY BEHIND SOCIAL TRANSMISSION

What really made you share was a desire to have someone else feel like you did when you discovered whatever it was you wanted to share. Human nature causes us all to want others to feel like us. Products and services that connect with us on an emotional level are the ones that get shared the most. As Wharton School marketing professor Jonah Berger puts it, "It's about the connection you build with your end user psychologically, functionally, personally, and emotionally." Companies are always striving to make products and services connect to their customers on this basis.

Any product or service can be emotional. Take, for example, one of the most ordinary products sold in the kitchenware section of every department store: the blender. Yes, the same blender that makes your smoothie of choice, favorite summer cocktail, and protein shake. The videos of the Blendtec product in action have become so viral and so talked about that chances are good that you've seen one and heard of the blender before reading this book. The marketing lesson here borders on being a classic. It's proof positive that any product can be remarkable. Any product can be emotional.

Here's the story: Blendtec is a company that produces commercial blending machines for use in homes, restaurants, smoothie shops, coffee shops, and more, all over the world. The product became popular in a huge way just as the smoothie craze began. It was truly the sharing of videos of this product in action that rocketed the company to stardom. The "Will It Blend" video phenomenon started when CEO Tom Dickson began testing the power and durability of the drive components in home blenders. With no budget and a video camera in hand, Dickson recorded demonstrations showing the blender blending the unexpected and put them on YouTube. The videos exploded in popularity almost overnight. Within the first five days, the videos were viewed more than six million times. To date, the blending videos have been viewed more than 100 million times.

Viewing videos is one thing, but what about people being motivated to take action as a result? Five years after the videos hit, retail sales have increased by more than 700 percent. I'd say that viewing and sharing worked. At first, the video that was most talked about was one showing an iPhone being pulverized into a pile of dust and powder. Telling someone the blender was powerful was one thing, but seeing it blend almost anything for real was what led to the explosion of Blendtec. The product truly was remarkable—the factor that gets products and services talked about most. Here are a few more reasons people talked about the Blendtec videos:

! *There were no limits imposed.* This implies a tremendous guarantee of performance, a primary characteristic of a remarkable product.

❗ *The story is easy to find and share.* Blendtec engages with their community on Twitter, Facebook, YouTube, their blog, and on a website.

❗ *What is being shown is unique and outrageous.* Add these components to a little humor and people will talk.

❗ *The product stands up to the test.* Marketing of a bad product always, of course, ends up a disaster. Marketing—especially in an outrageous fashion—a remarkable product ends up a resounding success.

Social sharing can exert tremendous influence, and thanks to technology it's more popular than ever, even if it has moved on from quilting circles and the Saturday morning coffee shop of yesteryear. It's now about technical amplification connecting humans to humans.

When you care about people, social sharing happens. People love to pass along anything that helps others avoid pain, sleep at night, or motivates them to go the extra mile. One of the immediate emotional connections that happened with the Blendtec blender demo was that the brand was humanized. Humanizing in marketing creates a connection on an emotional level. People do business with people, not icons, logos, or business names. Seeing that people behind a company are real and "just like us" gives the company the human voice and face needed to forge an emotional connection. In the Blendtec videos the CEO engages, uses humor, and is simply a real person.

Emotions should follow the marketing messaging. That means not holding back, talking about true feelings, not sugarcoating the negative, and not just showcasing the positive. The phrase "keep it real" is a good barometer of the emotional connection you're trying to strike in your own marketing messaging. The humans involved in the humanizing should not

MARKETING TRUTH

Emotional connections lead to social sharing and can lead to viral marketing.

sound like marketers at all. A customer should almost be able to forget that she is being marketed to when viewing a video, ad, or other content.

POPULARITY

Most dictionaries define popularity as "the state or condition of being liked, admired, or supported by many people." The real question is *why* things and people are liked, admired, and supported. Sometimes products, services, and ideas are popular simply because they are really, really good. If something tastes better, you like it more. If something helps you in your everyday life, you want to do it or have it. If you are entertained more by something, you will like it more and so will many others, making that form of entertainment popular.

There are other factors that contribute to popularity, too. Usually anything that will help people save time or money, avoid pain, or is more convenient will contribute to that product or service's popularity. In the world of marketing, these are the true *benefits* of products and services, not to be confused with *features*. Remember the marketing mantra we've mentioned before and asked you to keep in mind: "What's in it for me, the prospect?" If this question cannot be answered, it is not a benefit to your customer and it certainly won't contribute to popularity.

There is no doubt that popularity contributes to social sharing. We learned this when talking about the psychology behind social transmission. Popularity and social sharing influences significantly whether products, services, or ideas are bought or preferred. Preferred items become popular and are shared. That's exactly what happens with the whole notion of customer reviews, product critiques, and service recommendations, whether on- or offline.

According to the research firm Dimensional Research, 90 percent of consumers claimed that positive reviews influenced their decision to

---

MARKETING TRUTH

Popularity leads to social sharing.

---

buy. The corollary is also important to note: 86 percent of those surveyed said that *negative* reviews had influenced their buying decisions. Good or bad, reviews get noticed and are the essence of getting talked about. Since social sharing is done in a social community, the shared information is to a targeted audience.

Targeting your messages in a manner that is shared motivates a prospect to take action. Motivation happens right after engagement. Let's take a look at the world of engagement as it relates to getting noticed and remembered.

9

MUD ON THE WALL THAT STICKS: FROM ATTENTION TO ENGAGEMENT

Once you have someone's attention, then what? At that point the task becomes one of moving your prospect or target along a path toward engagement and action. This takes getting remembered and getting talked about. You need to nurture a prospect through the sales funnel to the point of buying. In the sales funnel you have to give prospects and customers a reason to contact you or take action to get more information. Once they have seen a consistent flow of information, they can choose to keep listening or figure out if your solution is right for them. It is at this point that you need to take the education of your prospect to a different level, moving to greater engagement and, in the case of the sales funnel, to the point of buying.

If you gain your audience's attention, you can continue to talk, inform, educate, and entertain them. If your audience is engaged, they'll be asking all of these things from you, pulling information from you, begging for more. That is why engagement is so important to the whole marketing process. Some would say that engagement is more important than attention, but that's like arguing whether the chicken or egg came first. They are both integral to successful marketing.

One way to move from attention to engagement is to communicate the benefits of what you have to say. Once people start hearing an answer to their (unspoken) question, "What's in it for me?" they'll seek more, which means they will engage with you more. Another path to engagement is to tease, fascinate, and create a sense of surprise or urgency along the way, after you've gotten their attention.

Third, having a message will engage people. This means you might have to state an opinion, speak passionately on a subject, or even stir up a bit of controversy. Controversy is engagement, not always the most desirable kind of engagement, but it typically means you are moving past the attention-getting point. As we've talked about, people like to listen to those they know, like, and trust. This means building rapport with those receiving your message. Not having a rapport will be a barrier to engagement. Social media guru Jason Falls says "Engagement is communicating well enough that the audience pays attention." You can nurture the attention that prospect is sharing with you by asking questions, agreeing or disagreeing, and presenting ideas and thoughts that he will find interesting, fresh, and relevant. Once that nurturing takes place, action happens—what all marketers want.

MARKETING TRUTH

Nurture the attention your prospect has given you by having conversations, asking questions, agreeing or disagreeing, and presenting ideas and thoughts that he will find interesting, fresh, and relevant.

TAGLINES

Part of getting remembered is related to how your product, service, or company is positioned. Positioning is what you do in the mind of a customer or prospect; it's perception. You've heard the saying that "perception is reality." We're talking here about positioning, or planting seeds of perception in the customer's or prospect's mind. Positioning can be done with marketing messaging, or with the look, feel, colors, logos, and taglines of your product or brand. A tagline is a phrase that advertisers create to visually implant in your mind the benefits, relevance, and position of products, services, people, or brands. Taglines are usually memorable and can help tie together the components of a brand's or campaign's identity.

Getting remembered with these taglines really boils down to delighting the imagination of your target prospects and customers, and characterizing whatever you are positioning in unique, original, and creative ways. Since the advent of commercial advertising, corporate taglines, ad slogans, and jingles have been used to penetrate our minds, create perceptions, make us remember, win our hearts, and motivate us to buy. Call them "brand bites," but they do influence marketing messaging, campaigns, and advertising.

Every marketer wants a catchy, memorable marketing or advertising message that will stick in their prospects' minds, help them position a product or service, and improve sales. The best taglines and slogans stick in people's minds, creating the top-of-mind awareness that every marketer dreams of. Some slogans and taglines that were introduced decades ago are still used and remembered to this day. Here are a few from the tagline hall of fame:

> "I'd walk a mile for a Camel." —Camel cigarettes
> "M'm! M'm! Good!" —Campbell's Soup
> "Please don't squeeze the Charmin." —Charmin toilet paper
> "Does she . . . or doesn't she?" —Clairol hair color
> "Plop, plop, fizz, fizz, oh what a relief it is!" —Alka-Seltzer antacid
> "You're in good hands with Allstate." —Allstate Insurance
> "Membership has its privileges." —American Express credit card
> "Don't leave home without it." —American Express credit card
> "When you care enough to send the very best." —Hallmark cards

"Nothing runs like a Deere." —John Deere tractors and machinery

"When it rains it pours." —Morton Salt

"Just do it." —Nike shoes

"Kills bugs dead." —Raid pesticide

"Strong enough for a man, but made for a woman." —Secret deodorant

"Takes a licking and keeps on ticking." —Timex watches

"Be all that you can be." —U.S. Army

"Can you hear me now?" —Verizon Wireless telecommunications company

"The document company." —Xerox photocopiers

"Let your fingers do the walking." —Yellow Pages directory

"The quicker picker-upper." —Bounty paper towels

"Say it with flowers." —FTD (Interflora)

"Look sharp, feel sharp." —Gillette razors

Pick the right marketing or advertising slogan and it will help you get and keep your prospects' attention. In some cases, that memory lasts long after your marketing campaign has ended and you've stopped selling the product.

One word of caution related to taglines and getting remembered: You never want to craft a confusing or unmemorable tagline, of course. Here are five thoughts on how to create one that sticks in your prospect's mind:

1. *Start by brainstorming a list of adjectives, action words, and benefits.* Then combine the words, rearrange them, and add to them to create phrases, slogans, and ideas. Once you've done that, let others take a look at your work and offer objective suggestions and new words and arrangements. Sleep on these overnight and repeat the process the following day. Your new tagline might hit you then, or you might think about it later and have an epiphany that hits you square between the eyes.

2. *Don't say too much.* Your tagline is not a billboard or website. It's designed to be short, catchy, and memorable, using just a few words or a tight phrase.

> ## MARKETING TRUTH
>
> *Taglines can position a business in the mind of a prospect by creating specific and memorable brand perceptions.*

3. *Don't be generic.* Tell your story and communicate your position and benefits, but don't be too bland. A tagline like "We Get Good Results" is boring and will not be associated with you nor remembered.

4. *Tell an emotional story.* That's what people connect with. Marketing still is a feeling and sensory discipline.

5. *Make your tagline functional.* It's OK to explain your product or service or its benefits. This is where you can communicate a unique competitive advantage. Find those adjectives and make a phrase out of it.

When thinking about your tagline, think succinct. Make it specific. Make it accurate. Make it true. Don't be global and general. Be narrow and specific. If your tagline is generic, abandon it. If it doesn't position you in a way that's different from the competition, ditch it. If it doesn't raise your friends' eyebrows, it isn't worth promoting to the public. Good taglines are the natural byproduct of a focused business model. That's where you must begin.

A tagline needs to say a lot with a little. Taglines should evolve with the company's marketing. They are not easy to create. Try one, test them, change them; it's OK. They can be a memorable touch to your target market. Get noticed, get remembered, and get talked about. That's my biggest marketing truth for you.

Your mind plays an important role when receiving marketing messages. There are ways to exercise the mind to keep it sharp, to tune it up, and to put it in a prime position to remember the marketing messages thrown at you. Let's look at your mind at work in the next chapter.

CHAPTER 10

YOUR MIND AT WORK: THE POWER OF MEMORY

C ATCHY JINGLES, SLOGANS, TAGLINES, AND OTHER MARKETING messages that bring back memories create lasting impressions. And lasting impressions are eventually talked about. The mind's capacity to store and recall information is truly a miracle, but memory doesn't always happen automatically or reliably. A few things to remember about memory:

❗ *Memory is contextual.* We typically don't, for example, memorize and recall a list of everyone we've ever met. We're likelier to think of cues, stories, and related events and a memory comes up.

❗ *Memory is stimulated by interest.* We are naturally likelier to recall something we're interested in, and less likely to do so if we're bored.

! *Visualization and imagination can spur memory recall.* Paint a picture in your prospect's mind (this is another way to explain visualization). Visualization includes visual and audio cues. Since memory is predominantly visual, this can be a powerful tool to tap into as a marketer.

! *Paying attention creates memories.* When you don't pay attention, memories are not formed, or the ones that are created are weak. Weak memories are harder to retrieve.

! *Jingles, lists, funny sayings, and mnemonic devices can make recall easier.* Remember the mnemonic device for recalling the colors of the rainbow? ROY G BIV, which stands for red, orange, yellow, green, blue, indigo, and violet. Make up your own: If you have to get milk, apples, and noodles at the grocery store, think of the "MAN" you have to buy.

! *Extreme visualizations and associations can help jog your memory, too.* If you have to go to the store to buy ice, think of opening the door of the store as you enter and tons of ice pouring out of the doorway to greet you. Other tricks for stimulating your prospects' memory and recall include summarizing what you're communicating to them along the way; repeating what you want them to remember; and encouraging them to write down, speak, or read important points.

There are many other memory-boosting techniques, of course. You can integrate some of these into your marketing messages, headlines, stories, websites, and advertisements.

MARKETING TRUTH

Memory works in marketing, and you can help encourage it in your prospects so they recall your brand and your messaging.

"CALL ME MAYBE"—CARLY RAE JEPSEN

The world, including *Billboard* magazine's "Hot 100 Chart," took notice when Carly Rae Jepsen introduced her mind-sticking ditty, "Call Me Maybe." Admit it; once you heard that song the repeat button got stuck in the "on" position in your head. It is the perfect embodiment of an "earworm."

An earworm is an involuntary piece of music that tunnels into your subconscious, planting securely in your brain. Every marketer would love to hear the exact combination of words that would allow them to create their own earworm, whether it's a song, jingle, headline, or tagline—that sound that prospects just can't get out of their head. Also known as "stuck song syndrome," this is a phenomenon of music psychology that we've all experienced, usually against our will. "Involuntary imagery of music is based on our skill to remember music, but for some reason feels out of control. But it is perfectly normal," says Lassi Liikkanen, a researcher at Helsinki Institute for Information Technology in Finland who has studied and written about earworms.

So what makes Jepsen's song an earworm? Why is it so catchy? What makes people notice it, then remember it, even if involuntarily? Here are a few things most earworms have in common:

! *Tempo.* "Call Me Maybe" is very similar to dance music and pop songs, usually around 120 beats per minute, the type of music people start tapping to or snapping their figures to.

! *Hook after hook after hook.* A simple hook might be a catchy melody or chorus that a listener sings along to repeatedly. By layering in catchy melodic sounds, as in this case, and snappy synthesizer strings, you get what's known as a "hook" in a song.

! *Simple notes.* Notes that don't have a lot of range, transitioning easily from one to the other, make a song easy to sing. Predictable rhymes and notes are pleasing to a listener and what make a song "catchy." Please the listener and they will notice and remember.

! *The lyrics are Dr. Seuss-like.* Simple, repeatable lyrics told in nursery rhyme fashion get noticed and certainly remembered.

Combining all these "sticky" components into one catchy package is easy; the challenge is getting the musical and lyrical balance. It has been said about "Call Me Maybe," even by the Jepsen camp, that there is no component of the song that is not super-catchy. All aspects of the song suck the listener in; it is the epitome of total engagement. Three minutes and 13 seconds of a catchy chorus, a melody that's easy on the ear, and lyrics simple enough to maintain a top-of-mind presence. All that, in addition to a song describing something that the song's primary target market (teen girls) can relate to, and you have a pop success: the ultimate earworm. James J. Kellaris, a professor of marketing at the University of Cincinnati who studies why certain songs are stickier than others, found that simplicity and repeatability are crucial to a song's catchiness. Chances are, right now "Call Me Maybe" is bouncing around your head.

You are not the only one that can help make that message stick in your prospect's mind. The market is cluttered. It's cluttered because others want your space. Those "others" are competitors. Let me share with you how to take advantage of competitors and what they are doing with their messaging.

MARKETING TRUTH

"Stuck song syndrome," like getting any message stuck in your mind, is a good thing when wanting to get noticed, remembered, and talked about.

TAKING ADVANTAGE OF COMPETITION

RICHARD BRANSON, THE FAMED FOUNDER OF VIRGIN AIRLINES (among other Virgin brands), is very competitive. So when British Airways scored a marketing coup by landing sponsorship of the London Eye, the massive Ferris wheel on the banks of the Thames River in London, it's safe to say that Branson was none too happy.

To announce the sponsorship, British Airways (BA) called a press conference. On the day of the press conference, however, there was a problem raising the London Eye: It was literally lying on the ground next to its supporting structure. Virgin sprang into action to take advantage of this *faux pas*. In short order, they had arranged for a large blimp, complete with a printed message on its side: "BA can't get it up."

Virgin flew the airship over the grounded ferris wheel at the time of the press conference and ended up getting more coverage than the press conference itself. Richard Branson was quoted as saying, "This is the stuff that makes people smile. It is done in a tongue-in-cheek way, but it is very much part of the Virgin brand. It is this kind of fun, spirited competition that helps build a brand." Needless to say, his marketing action got noticed and talked about.

In the automotive world, car brands compete head on with each other. Sometimes it's one against many and sometimes it's one on one. Head-on, one-on-one competition was evident in a recent billboard war between the luxury brands Audi vs. BMW.

At a busy Los Angeles intersection (Santa Monica and Beverly Glen Boulevards), Audi placed a billboard to promote their near-luxury A4 sedan. The billboard simply was a photo of their car, visually attractive, with the simple message/tagline stating, "Your move, BMW."

In the nearby town of Santa Monica, a competitive auto dealership, mainly selling BMW's, bought advertising space on an adjacent billboard. That billboard featured an equally appealing photo of the competitive BMW M3 near-luxury sedan. Their tagline, ingeniously crafted and placed, was one simple word, "Checkmate."

This was the start of a mini-billboard war. Audi went on the social media warpath with a Facebook page encouraging their followers to contribute their own innovative advertising slogans. Interested fans took part with contributions of slogans such as, "Chess? I'd rather be driving."

Messages were communicated in good, competitive spirit. The automotive market is a very competitive environment. Both brands consider these kinds of marketing moves to defend their leadership positions and to continue to stay top of mind with their target market. The checkmate billboard got talked about. Audi and BMW were both mentioned in the ensuing discussions.

MARKETING TRUTH

Fun, spirited competition helps build a brand.

When *Forbes* magazine reported on this, they stated, "There's something about our incredible capitalist system that doesn't simply breed competition, it inspires acts of war—marketing war to be precise."

BMW saw an opening and they grabbed it. Marketing is all around. You just have to look. BMW looked and they capitalized. That's the spirit of good competition. That's how you get talked about.

Richard Branson and BMW thought about their brands unconventionally to reach their conventional business goals. Guerrilla marketing is unconventional marketing methods to reach conventional marketing goals. You will be glad to read the next chapter with a conventional mindset but using unconventional ideas.

12

GUERRILLA MARKETING

JUST LOOK AROUND AT ALL THE MARKETING COMING YOUR WAY. There are signs, radio commercials, point-of-purchase displays, labels, offers in your mail, TV ads, magazines, salespeople, online advertising, and on and on and on. Add all these up and the number of marketing pieces you're exposed to every day usually amounts to more than 5,000. Walk into a grocery store and this number doubles.

All these headlines offer something of value to an interested prospect. They'll all increase not only the attention your pieces get but your response rates as well. As you craft your call to action, you need to answer the following questions:

❗ What is the purpose of your marketing efforts this time around?

❗ What do you want people to do as a result of your marketing?

! What action do you want recipients to take?

After you've answered these questions, you'll have a better idea of what hooks your pieces should contain, which will help you design your pieces. For example, if you're using print marketing to communicate to your target market, put these hooks in a starburst graphic. If it's in an audio or video format, make it extreme, loud, and memorable.

Standing out in the marketing clutter will always be a marketer's challenge. Doing it in guerrilla fashion will always be a marketer's solution. The underlying goal of guerrilla marketing is to reach conventional marketing goals with unconventional methods and do so in an efficient way so that you aren't spending and wasting big bucks along the way.

IKEA got into the guerrilla marketing game with their Bondi Beach Bookshelf. The Swedish furniture maker learned through a little guerrilla marketing research that one-third of all Australians would, if they could, spend an extra hour reading a good book. In honor of the 30th anniversary of the company's most popular bookshelf, IKEA set up the world's largest outdoor library on Bondi Beach using the best-selling bookshelf. Not only did it get noticed, it got used. It was unconventional. It was out-of-the-box. It was on the beach. IKEA lined up enough bookshelves on Bondi Beach to hold 6,000 books. Those passing by could take one, exchange it for one of their own, or make a donation to the Australian Literacy and Numeracy Foundation. Who would have thought?

Taco Bell got into guerrilla marketing action in March 2001, when the Russian spaceship Mir was circling the earth. When Russian spaceships re-enter the earth post-mission, they more or less, eject the cosmonaut and let the pieces of the spaceship fall to earth. Taco Bell got wind of that and created a 40 –by-40-foot target painted with a Bell bull's eye and big bold purple letters announcing, "Free Taco Here." Taco Bell took their target ten miles off the coast of Australia and threw it into the Pacific Ocean and stood back and awaited the spaceship's descent. They then announced and offered a free taco to everyone in America if the spaceship pieces hit their water-borne target.

Taco Bell used guerrilla marketing or unconventional marketing to achieve the conventional marketing goal of awareness. Taco Bell generated millions of dollars of PR, marketing, and awareness by using a little bit of time, a little bit of energy, and a whole lot of imagination, which are the underlying principles of guerrilla marketing. Taco Bell not only gained market share in the fast food industry. they also got noticed and captured the imagination of America as that spaceship descended. To this day people remember that marketing. (Note: The pieces of the spaceship finally did land ten miles off of the coast of the country of Chile. Taco Bell gained attention with guerrilla marketing and didn't have to fulfill their offer.)

The same guerrilla marketing approach can happen with small-business marketing, which often is local. Take AIM Electrical and Plumbing, located in Halifax, Nova Scotia, Canada. They basically painted the outside driver's door to look like the driver's torso is sitting on a toilet. Talk about getting noticed! Talk about getting remembered and mostly— talk about getting talked about—this visual does all three. Most people take a picture, especially in today's world of mobile smartphones. People remember and call this business—as they market like they mean it.

These examples are only the tip of the imaginative marketing iceberg. There are many more examples and success stories. Guerrilla marketing, with its out-of-the-box tactics, is really all about winning the battle for attention and coming up with ideas that will be remembered by your prospects and customers. Put on your thinking cap; sometimes it's just about a couple of quick points to achieve those marketing goals:

! *Use your physical surroundings to gain attention.* Challenge the status quo, even if it's just writing messages in chalk on a sidewalk or putting a cardboard frame around a car mirror. Be bold, extreme, outrageous, unafraid, and take a chance. Let your target market tell you what fits this formula, what will turn their head, or what will make them gasp.

! *Offer a customer service experience that is so outstanding that your customers can't help but spread the word like wildfire.* Many call this "the WOW factor," or "the aha! moment." People like to talk about fun and exciting experiences; that's the essence of sharing.

! *Go ahead and be extreme to get attention.* If it scares you to do it, it's probably worth doing if getting noticed and talked about is your marketing goal.

Chapter 12 / Guerrilla Marketing

! *Use unconventional thinking* and means to achieve conventional marketing goals of awareness, buzz, and stickiness.

! Instead of writing checks for marketing that might or might not work, use time, energy, imagination, information, and knowledge to leverage your ideas and burst into the minds of your prospects.

Guerrilla marketing is only limited by the imagination you put forth. Whether conventional or unconventional, you have now learned how to get remembered right after getting noticed. The more you remember, the more you share. This sharing is the key marketing component of getting talked about, and now we will take a look at that.

MARKETING TRUTH

Guerrilla marketing is a way of reaching conventional marketing goals with unconventional methods and doing so efficiently. Imagination is key here, not big bucks.

GET TALKED

ABOUT

CHAPTER 13

INFLUENCE
MARKETING

I F A CUSTOMER BUYS YOUR PRODUCT ONCE AND NEVER TELLS ANYONE about it, you have marketed one time, to one person, and are done. That is clearly totally inefficient marketing. But if a customer buys your product once and they tell 1,000 people about it and 10 percent of those people buy your product, and those people tell others about it, you have just marketed many times to many people. That is very efficient marketing and the kind of marketing every business and organization wants. This level of efficiency only happens when people talk about a product, company, person, or service. This only happens when there is sufficient word-of-mouth marketing and/or marketing buzz.

Marketing buzz is defined as the interaction of consumers of a product or service that serves to amplify the original marketing message. Word-of-mouth marketing, buzz marketing, and getting anything talked about works because individuals are trusted more than are organizations talking about their own products and services. More than 90 percent of consumers say they trust word-of-mouth marketing and recommendations from peers, family members, and friends more than all other forms of advertising. This statistic has skyrocketed in recent years because of the web, social media marketing, and other types of technology that are now at the forefront of effective marketing. And unless you're blessed with a blank check to spend on marketing, you want marketing efficiency.

Another term for this is "influencer marketing." Influencer marketing is red-hot today, with most of that influence coming from peers in social media communities.

Business success happens when there are lots of mutually beneficial relationships built. These are individual connections. Connections give access and expand geometrically. Many times this area of influence is referred to as the sphere of influence. Most successful businesses consider their sphere a major business asset. This sphere of influence is key in getting marketing messages communicated and motivating prospects to take action.

I hope you're seeing a lot of what you've learned in this book come together, building on getting noticed to getting remembered and now getting talked about.

Consumer, meet product and service. Product and service, meet consumer. Go ahead and spread the word. Welcome to the world of influence. Also, welcome to the world of marketing buzz. Buzz happens. Not sure about that? Take a look at the next chapter and you will see buzz in action.

CHAPTER 14

BUZZ
HAPPENS

I T'S UNLIKELY THAT YOU'VE MISSED ONE OF THE BIGGEST, BADDEST, hottest examples of getting noticed and catapulted into top-of-mind awareness. Justin Bieber not only got noticed and remembered, but people are still talking about him several years later. Unfortunately, because of some recent, socially unacceptable behavior and childish antics by Beiber, his notoriety is drifting negative. Despite young Bieber's implosion, there are still marketing questions to be learned from asking how did Justin Bieber get discovered;, how did he get noticed, and how did he keep the buzz going?

JUSTIN BIEBER GETS NOTICED

Let's back up a bit: Beiber is clearly one of the most famous singing sensations of his generation. He has had some of the most successful record launches and concerts around the world, with hits like "Baby" and "One Time." What's the story behind his success? Beiber was born and raised in a small Canadian town just west of Toronto, Ontario. Born to a single mom, he was raised in government-subsidized housing, and like many other small-town kids, he entertained himself by imitating music stars, eventually teaching himself to play the piano, guitar, drums, and other instruments. At the age of 12 he entered a local talent show and won second place for his rendition of Ne-Yo's "So Sick." This performance and others were posted on YouTube by his mom. "It had a hundred views, then 1,000 views, then 10,000 views," Beiber reported, so he just kept posting more videos.

During this time, Scooter Braun, a 30-something Atlanta party promoter, was researching an unrelated YouTube sensation for singer Akon and accidentally happened upon one of Beiber's videos. Braun knew talent when he heard it; Beiber's tone and range were unique, especially for a 12-year-old. Braun sought out the young boy, found his mother, and invited them to visit Atlanta for a live audition. Braun had also invited superstar Usher to the audition. Usher heard the audition and instantly recognized a star. He contacted fellow music producer L.A. Reid, the owner of Island Records, and eventually signed Beiber to the label.

Usher himself was launched from obscurity to stardom with the help of the TV show *Star Search*; Usher's new protégé, Justin Bieber, had YouTube. In 2009, Beiber's very first song, "One Time," landed him in the Top 30 charts in more than ten countries. This was followed soon thereafter by a debut album that was certified platinum in the U.S. Seven songs from that album simultaneously landed in the Billboard Hot 100.

So why did the buzz about Justin Bieber continue? What continues to fuel the marketing buzz? Justin Bieber reached out. He first used YouTube to share his music. His YouTube videos were noticed, and then his producers kept on using the platform to promote his music. Beiber was a believer, as was his management, that he could reach more fans by uploading more videos to YouTube. Bieber also used Twitter to interact with fans and supporters, as well as cultivating his presence on Facebook. In less than three months he had amassed more than one million Twitter followers. Beiber also was an early adopter of Instagram: Nearly two million people follow Beiber there.

Whether it seems like it or not, there was truly hard work at play here. That, along with finding a distribution venue like YouTube to showcase Beiber's talents, spelled success for the pop star; today it still continues to feed his marketing buzz, and he is a global brand and a pop icon. "It used to be there was a mystery to the artist," said Beiber. "Now there's, like, no mystery—the fans want the connection, they want to see you Instagramming at a coffee shop in the morning." Today Beiber claims more than 49 million Twitter followers—more than any person on earth except Lady Gaga. The video for his breakout debut song, "Baby," has had more than 740 million views on YouTube, making it the most-watched video in YouTube history. Jack Flannery, writing for Rise Interactive, a digital marketing agency that specializes in traffic generation and web analytics, put it best: "He's got a great voice, 'pretty hair,' and caters to a fan base so diehard they've been known to riot at the slightest provocation or promise of a mall appearance." Social media marketing is what Justin Bieber does absolutely right; more than 49 million Twitter followers, 55 million Facebook Likes, and a total of nearly three billion YouTube views afford him a gargantuan social influence that big-name brands strive for. Like other stars, he has the backing of a major record label, but his real power is in the fact that he continues to engage and share in social media communities with his fans.

Here are a few marketing truths related to how Justin Bieber gets noticed and talked about:

! Two-way communication with fans and prospective fans. Beiber knows two-way conversation and sharing are necessary. His postings are not one-way shouts of things that are all about him. He asks his followers to share their days with him and asks them questions.

MARKETING TRUTH

Engaging, interacting, and sharing in social media communities can build a huge fan base.

- ! Providing fans with a personal, insider view of his life
- ! Continuing to build trust and loyalty through his intense, consistent engagement with fans
- ! Cross-marketing YouTube with Twitter, Facebook, and Instagram

BEATS™ BY DR. DRE™

Starbucks achieved a marketer's dream. They took a cup of coffee and turned it into a premium brand experience. No one would have predicted that customers would pay $4 for a simple cup of coffee, especially with fast-food competitors selling coffee for a dollar or less. Starbucks created a brand experience by getting noticed, remembered, and talked about. In a single year Starbucks sells four billion cups of this commodity product.

Just like the introduction of expensive coffee, only a few would have believed that thousands of people would consider spending $300 on headphones. Thanks to the involvement of a hip-hop legend and a few other music gurus, headphones costing several hundreds of dollars have become one of the fastest-growing categories in the consumer electronics industry. It's safe to say, in fact, that the premium headphone market has exploded. Not only do premium headphones make up more than 40 percent of all headphone sales, but those buying them have, on average, more than one pair. Of that premium headphone market, Beats™ by Dr. Dre™, the company founded by hip-hop artist Dr. Dre and music producer Jimmy Iovine, have a market share of more than 60 percent. All this is attributable to a new way of thinking about music marketing and customer experience. You can bet that when the first pair was put on the market for $300, people called them crazy.

One factor driving the premium headphone market is the proliferation of smartphones and tablets that make huge music collections portable. As more consumers enjoy listening to their music on these devices, headphones become the logical hardware extension of their experience. This extension, plus the drive for all technology to achieve a new level of performance, affected the acceptance of premium headphones as well.

Beats by Dr. Dre was at the right place to answer this need at the right time. Timing aside, Beats by Dr. Dre also got noticed and talked about because they were successful in making headphones as much a fashion accessory as a listening device. Walking around with these headphones around your neck or on your ears told the world that music was a part of your life and that you wanted the best-sounding music possible. They became status symbols. It was a marketing home run.

Jimmy Iovine's goal for the headphones sounds simple: "Let's make it look cool and have a good vibe about it, yet make it powerful." Accessorizing with the headphones became part of the hottest musicians' music videos. Sports celebrities were shown walking off their team buses and in their locker rooms wearing Beats by Dr. Dre. Instead of celebrity endorsements, Beats by Dr. Dre had celebrity *use*, from the likes of Justin Bieber, Lady Gaga, and LeBron James, all of which helped propel acceptance of the premium headphones, which translated into product demand and sales. In short, Beats by Dr. Dre redefined the earbud and headphone market. The red "b" logo became iconic, and the accessory became a must-have for millions of young people. Beats redefined how much people were willing to pay for a pair of headphones, and they did it even during lean economic times. Stephanie Reichert, vice president of strategic marketing for Sennheiser USA, a distributor of premium audio products, observed that Beats by Dr. Dre was the first to market headphones as a lifestyle choice rather than a piece of audio equipment.

Their strategy boils down to enchanting the public. Traditional marketing and consumer education was deemed too long-term-oriented for this product. The decision was made to make Beats by Dr. Dre the hottest product to have. The exceptional sound was just thrown in as an aside. It worked. Consumers now spend $500 million a year on something that sounds good, but also makes them look cool along the way. Looking cool definitely gets noticed, remembered, and talked about—and Beats by Dr. Dre definitely look cool.

MARKETING TRUTH

Creating a status symbol is a marketing home run!

RELEVANCE

You've read already in this book several times that communicating with your consumers and prospects using fresh, interesting, and relevant content gets noticed, remembered, and talked about. We've discussed being interesting. Now let's talk about being relevant. The term *relevance*, especially in the worlds of social media and content, has risen to the top, right up there with *transparency* and *community*. Right from the get-go, unless you deliver information, an offer, entertainment, or something that speaks *directly* to the receiver of the content, they won't care about your communication. In today's content-heavy, marketing-cluttered world, people are protective of their time and attention and won't give it to something they find irrelevant. Messages and information get tuned out quicker today than they used to because consumers of information have learned to sort through content instantly. That instantaneous sorting starts with relevance. The whole concept of targeting begins with being relevant. Send information and messages to the right target, and chances are good that it will be consumed. That's relevance. Send information and messages to the wrong target, and the chance of consumption drops to zero. That's irrelevance.

So the question is, how do marketers break through that clutter? How can you turn content, messages, and information into relevance? Let's take a look at four key points:

1. *It's all about the consumer of your content, not you.* All they care about when reading your content is, "What does this have to do with me? What's in it for me? How is this relevant to me, my problems, my opportunities, or my situation?" Other questions related to this might be, "Why is this important? Why must I learn this?" Start with the intent of answering all these questions; that's the key to creating and delivering relevant content. In terms of the branding component of marketing, it is rooted in establishing credibility, building trust, increasing relevance, and driving action.

2. *Loyalty and trust matter when you're delivering content.* "If I liked you before and if you were relevant before, chances are you will be relevant to me again." If you recognize the sender of content, they are more likely to be relevant to you. Similarly, if someone sends

you irrelevant information, chances are you'll remember that, too. By appealing to my interests, past behavior, and specific opportunities I want to know about, you increase the likelihood of interaction, engagement, and potential conversion.

3. *Talking to your target (rather than to a very broad or mass audience) improves relevance.* Target markets are made up of those that match a certain set of characteristics, values, beliefs, demographics, and more. Using data to develop these targets increases the probability of relevance. Precise and accurate targeting is easier to do today thanks to the big marketing and purchasing behavior data that's available.

4. *It's all about relationships.* We've said this before, but relevance is key for relationship-building and maintenance that motivates people to take action in the form of buying. If you don't have an offer or a mission of relevance, you need to use relationship-building as a way to establish the trust and confidence that is a function of relevance.

One more fact to consider is that the word *relevance* is built into the definition of content marketing, as defined by the Content Marketing Institute. The organization states in their definition that "content marketing is a marketing technique of creating and distributing *relevant* and valuable content to attract, acquire, and engage a clearly defined and understood target audience, with the objective of driving profitable customer action." They go on to say that "content marketing's purpose is to attract and retain customers by consistently creating and curating *relevant* and valuable content with the intention of changing or enhancing consumer behavior."

In today's world of online marketing and ecommerce, that action is buying. Customers are becoming more sophisticated in their product research and shopping habits. If they have a good experience as they search, they will expect the same type of experience when shopping. Ensuring the utmost relevance will meet or exceed consumers' expectations, resulting in a delightful search and shopping experience. This also applies to "shopping" in the B2B world, where shopping could be a comparison analysis between two different solutions.

MARKETING TRUTH

"Content marketing is the marketing technique of creating and distributing relevant and valuable content to attract, acquire, and engage a clearly defined and understood target audience—with the objective of driving profitable customer action."

—Content Marketing Institute

Earlier we used trust in the description of relevance. As a marketer you are trying to foster a cohesive and active community by establishing trust and being believable—all cornerstones for relevance. Content is definitely king, but relevance rules!

WORD-OF-MOUTH MATTERS

According to the *McKinsey Quarterly*, "Word-of-mouth generates more than twice the sales of paid advertising in categories as diverse as skin care and mobile phones." Marketing is not always all about spending a lot of money on elaborate campaigns. What often persuades consumers into buying is something simpler and less costly than most campaigns: word-of-mouth recommendations from a trusted source. It's already been stated here that you are bombarded every day by many marketing messages, with most of these coming at you in the form of traditional marketing. Word-of-mouth is effective because it clearly cuts through the marketing clutter, many times with great impact.

McKinsey goes on to report that word-of-mouth is the primary factor behind 20 to 50 percent of all purchasing decisions. Word-of-mouth is highly influential when consumers have a reason to do research, as with a costly purchase. In this case, recommendations from a trusted friend or peer weigh out over traditional advertising. Social sharing and communication have accelerated word-of-mouth communication to the point where it is mass communication to communities versus the old days of one-on-one communication. Product reviews, customer experiences, and recommendations are posted online and opinions are all shared through social networks. That stands out many times over traditional advertising that may or may not be seen or may or may not be paid attention to.

Thanks to the internet, word-of-mouth marketing is on steroids with the help of social media, blogs, podcasts, video, content marketing, commenting, and more.

I told you you would see buzz in action. Imagine buzz on steroids. That's what happens when you introduce buzz into social communities. Communities are in full display and review in the next chapter.

MARKETING TRUTH

Product reviews, customer experiences, and recommendations are posted online and opinions are shared through social networks. Word-of-mouth marketing very often stands out over traditional advertising.

CHAPTER 15

IT TAKES A ~~VILLAGE~~ COMMUNITY

ILLARY CLINTON WROTE A BOOK, *IT TAKES A VILLAGE*, THAT focuses on the impact individuals and groups outside the family have on a child's well-being and advocates for a society that helps to meet all of a child's needs. Our society is an extended village. And the same concept applies in today's world of social media marketing, although the word "village" can be substituted with "community." In order to effectively market using social media marketing, it obviously takes a community. Many times, it now takes social media marketing and online communities to get noticed and to fuel the marketing buzz necessary for products to be remembered and to gain a top-of-mind awareness position.

Social communities are essentially a collection that allows for participation and influence. One advantage of communities over advertising is the ability to spot and engage the most influential individuals within a given social community. There are also advantages related to creating and growing a community around a cause, person, product, company, or organization, while letting the digital conversations come to life with participants and those who can be influenced. You can see this in action in LinkedIn groups, business pages on Facebook, or popular blogs with active followings, like CopyBlogger.com or Hubspot.com.

Kurt Vonnegut, the American novelist and essayist, was ahead of his time when he asked in the 1960s, "What should young people do with their lives today? Many things, obviously. But the most daring thing is to create stable communities in which the terrible disease of loneliness can be cured." This situation and advice still exists today. Johann Wolfgang von Goethe, a German writer and politician in the 18th and 19th centuries, was ahead of his time of well. This is what he said about community: "The world is so empty if one thinks only of mountains, rivers, and cities; but to know someone who thinks and feels with us, and who, though distant, is close to us in spirit, this makes the earth for us an inhabited garden." A bit more flowery than Vonnegut, but essentially the same message. Technology is clearly allowing new kinds of connections and communities to be created today.

Those who are part of a community are many times there to be influenced and inspired. Encouraging people to connect builds effective communities. Part of connecting within a community is the sense of belonging, but there's also a sense of the power of the masses. The more you connect and help community members achieve their goals, the more you will achieve yours. Give before you get. You've probably heard this before, but in communities it is true. Encourage, help, and connect with others and you truly have a community.

Today it very often takes an online community to effectively communicate messages en masse. Businesses and organizations need to integrate social media marketing and community participation into all other marketing efforts in order to spread their word once they have gotten noticed. This includes content marketing, communication related

---

MARKETING TRUTH

It takes social media marketing and online communities to get noticed and to fuel the marketing buzz necessary for products to be remembered and to gain a top-of-mind awareness position.

---

to lead generation, website traffic, and anything related to increasing revenues.

Tell one person, and you have a conversation. Tell many, and not only do you have a community, you have a potential virus. A marketing virus reaches many and is a good thing. Look at the fuel that made the next items go viral on the way to getting remembered and certainly talked about.

CHAPTER

16

WHY VIDEOS
GO VIRAL

KEVIN ALLOCCA IS YOUTUBE'S TRENDS MANAGER. AT A RECENT
TED Talk, Allocca shared reasons why videos go viral. He offers
the following factors:

! *Tastemakers.* This is a term that Allocca gave to those who
introduce us to new and interesting things and bring them to a
new and larger audience. It could be something shared on a late-
night TV show or a feature article on a site like Mashable.com.

! *Community participation.* A community typically forms
around a shared interest or something else a group has in
common. The participants may start talking about a video
and word takes off. We don't just enjoy viral videos, we

participate in the communities that talk about them and very often help spread the word.

! *Videos that are totally surprising.* This almost goes without saying, but many of the videos you share are completely unexpected in some way.

WESTJET

Let's see Allocca's observations in action. WestJet, a Canadian airline company whose mission is to provide safe, friendly, and affordable air travel, produced a very memorable video for the 2013 Christmas season. They called it their "Christmas Miracle" video. From Day One, it won the attention of their target market; within the first ten days, the video was viewed almost 30 million times.

The video shows holiday travelers talking with a live Santa through a TV screen surrounded by a large gift box. Santa asks every passenger what their Christmas gift wish is. The passengers answer Santa, then board the plane for their two-hour flight to western Canada. While the plane is en route to its destination, WestJet employees go shopping for the items mentioned by the passengers, wrap the gifts, and add a personal gift tag with the name of each customer, ready to deliver their gift at baggage claim.

Upon arrival, the travelers wait for their luggage at baggage claim, and after a fanfare of Christmas music and the dropping of confetti, one by one, the gifts appear on the luggage conveyor. Needless to say, the passengers were shocked and delighted to find exactly what they asked for, wrapped and ready at baggage claim! WestJet filmed the whole surprise and went public with the video shortly thereafter. The "Christmas Miracle" soon went viral. Here are some takeaways from WestJet's marketing bonanza:

! *The video reflected the employee-owned company's culture, identity, and values, especially putting customers first.* WestJet is the Southwest Airlines of the north. They have fun. They treat passengers like family members, and their service to customers comes first. WestJet publicly states that their brand is all about being fun and caring. This video reinforced that.

! *Marketing can be entertaining without being commercial.* WestJet knew the entertainment value would drive the buzz and the buzz would take care of the marketing. When watching the video, you lose sight of the commercial intent. The video is funny, fun, and filled with holiday feeling. You can't help but feel warm when watching the video. Associating these feelings with the brand is something that a print ad can't convey.

MARKETING TRUTH

A well-executed campaign should combine a number of marketing truths: entertainment, warmth, staying true to the brand, and not being overly commercial.

A CATCHPHRASE IS BORN: "AIN'T NOBODY GOT TIME FOR THAT"

An Oklahoma woman known as "Sweet Brown," aka Kimberly Wilkins, found internet fame after KFOR-TV in Oklahoma City interviewed her after her apartment caught fire. Kimberly Wilkins definitely got talked about.

Complete with the traditional knotted multicolored head scarf and spouting furiously with a thick accent, Brown described, with her own dramatic flair, the horrific experience of seeing her apartment complex on fire. Her honesty and ability to speak on camera without a care created a twist to the story that viewers were not expecting. Her theatrical diatribe entered the YouTube space as she was introduced to millions upon millions (and now billions) of viewers.

In the original story, she took 40 seconds to tell the reporter her account: "Well, I woke up to go get me a cold pop, and then I thought somebody was barbecuin' and I said oh, Lord, oh, Jesus, it's a fire. Then I ran out, I didn't grab no shoes or nothin,' Jesus. I ran for my [expletive deleted] life, and then the smoke got me. I got bronchitis. Ain't nobody got time for that."

Chapter 16 / Why Videos Go Viral

People immediately shared her story, her video, her picture, and their own recounts of her outburst on Facebook, Twitter, YouTube, and elsewhere. Wilkins has what was termed a "musical" accent that led to many remixes of her video clip, causing it to spread even more. Two lines in particular—"I got bronchitis" and "Ain't nobody got time for that"— spawned plenty of foot-tapping remixes. The invitations soon rolled in for TV appearances, including one for ABC's *The View*.

What made it get noticed? What made it remembered? Why did people spread the story and talk about it so much? There are a lot of factors at work here. Sweet Brown was honest, excited, and passionate about telling her story and didn't care about polish, grammar, or what the world thought about her description. She used everyday language and threw in a line that turned into a catchphrase: "Ain't nobody got time for that." It had a dose of humor and was totally unexpected. Take all that and add it to the following and you have a viral formula:

! *Mentioned by Beyoncé at the Super Bowl.* You want a catchphrase to catch on, get Beyoncé to recite the line at the Super Bowl. You can't script things like this, but you know the numbers. Beyoncé has that golden touch and people definitely talked about Beyoncé and Sweet Brown that night.

! *Sweet Brown is a survivor.* It was a fire in the middle of the night and many people were seriously injured in that fire. But Sweet Brown made it out safely; she was a survivor. Everybody likes the story of a survivor and talks about it.

! *We can relate to her.* Sweet Brown is funny, real, and uses real-world language. She had a carefree approach to a serious situation. We all know someone like her.

! A catchphrase was catapulted. The phrase "Ain't nobody got time for that" applies to a whole lot of situations. You still hear people using this phrase, in fact. It not only caught on and spread, it has stuck.

Look up Sweet Brown online and you'll see her described as a YouTube celebrity. We all have the possibility of our "15 minutes of fame," as Sweet Brown had—the chance to be in a video that's shared and talked about by millions.

MARKETING TRUTH

A catchphrase that sticks, spreads, catches on is remembered and talked about.

Note: Not that it affects the point in this book, but as a point of fact, in April 2013 Sweet Brown sued Apple for selling a song called "I Got Bronchitis" on iTunes for profit, using catchphrases uttered by her in the video, such as "Ain't nobody got time for that," "Ran for my life," and "Oh, Lord Jesus, it's a fire."

VIRAL THOUGHTS

Someone contacted me the other day and asked me to create something for them that would go viral. If going viral were that easy, there would never be another marketing challenge. Unfortunately for marketers, going viral is not just a matter of flipping a marketing switch. There is no set formula that is guaranteed to work. There are some things that have a higher probability of going viral, however, compared to others. There is a bit of science behind the reasons why people share content, and there are some fundamentals that viral content does share.

When I was first asked to construct something that could go viral, my mind immediately thought back to all those things I have personally shared and laughed at, the things that I wanted to make sure others enjoyed as much as I did. These include:

! Anything related to babies and cute kids
! Extreme things: the biggest, fastest, stupidest, noisiest, most obnoxious, etc.
! Humor
! Animals: unusual, cute, ones we don't see often, animal tricks, etc.
! Goofiness (aka stupid things)
! Sex (There. I said it. I'm not talking about pornography, but anything related to sex and sexiness; not including the act of.)

! Games, quizzes, contests, competitions

Take a look at videos you've watched lately. Then think about the ones you wanted others to see to share in your laughter, amazement, and enjoyment. Virality can't happen without sharing. Instead of trying to determine what will go viral, think first, what do people want to share?

Let's look at some other things that are highly shareable:

! The use of a #hashtag on Twitter, Instagram, or Facebook
! "Before and after" stories, usually related to a product or service
! Holiday content, whether it's a mainstream holiday, a birthday or other celebration, or a holiday that you make up that is unusual or clever
! Valuable, downloadable content: a PDF, ebook, article, or special report, or any other information of value
! Controversial discussion, issues, or news
! Emotional, tear-jerker stories, reunions, special needs situations
! Memorable: this is tough to define, because *memorable* means different things to different people.
! Charitable or heroic feats of significance
! Celebrity bloggers, tweeters, and videos (non-commercial)
! Key influencers, including semi-celebrities

In the online world and specifically in social media communities, we want interaction. That is the essence of social media. That interaction may take the form of sharing an experience, good or bad, within that defined community. People like to share personal experiences.

Sometimes people have an incentive to share something. That incentive might be monetary or materialistic or it may be a personal reward that is received simply by sharing. If I share content about this book, my incentive is that more books will be sold. People share things they want associated with them, their brand, identity, or positioning. This is a form of recognition. The more things you offer as a marketer that help your customers or prospects look good, the higher the probability that they will engage with you and share. This association also can take the form of citing a brand, product, company, service, or personal preference.

> ## MARKETING TRUTH
>
> *Understanding what motivates people to share will contribute to the*
> *potential of your marketing message going viral.*

If you want to get talked about, figure out what people—especially your target market—share the most and why, and apply these findings to help your marketing messages achieve virality.

Viral messages can go from anyone to anyone. Imagine when friends are involved. Messages are solidified and more effective when going from one friend to another. In the next chapter friends are involved in very creative ways.

CHAPTER 17

TELLING
FRIENDS

WHETHER IT MADE YOU CRY OR MADE YOU BUY THE PRODUCT it advertised, Guinness produced a commercial with a marketing message that definitely got talked about and remembered. Every guy I talked to about it mentioned that they not only saw it but they shared it with friends and family. The YouTube views for the commercial soared to more than three million views almost overnight.

GUINNESS WHEELCHAIR BASKETBALL

In the commercial, a group of fit, athletic men play an intense, adrenaline-charged, rough-and-tumble game of wheelchair basketball in the local gym. Touching, emotional, heart-tugging music fills the background. Three-quarters of the way into the commercial, sweat flying, chairs colliding, five of the six men stand up and walk out of the gym, wheelchairs left behind. Accompanying them is the lone true wheelchair-bound athlete and they're all headed out together for their pint of Guinness. As viewers we then understand that the able-bodied men joined their handicapped friend in wheelchairs to remove disability from their match and so that everyone could engage in a fair athletic contest. No one watching the commercial saw that coming. The ad ends with a scene of the men enjoying a pint of Guinness at a bar as a voiceover intones: "Dedication. Loyalty. Friendship. The choices we make reveal the true nature of our character." Congratulations, Guinness.

The beer maker masterfully combined brawn with sensitivity, not only knocking it out of the advertising park, but separating themselves from the pack, their competitors. They did this by showing a brand of masculinity that other beer advertisers don't show. Why did this commercial and its message hit the heart? Why did it go viral? Why did it get talked about at every water cooler the day after it aired? The answers to these questions are key to understanding what it takes to get noticed, remembered, and talked about.

Here are a few considerations as to why this ad was so powerful and successful:

> ! *A surprising plot twist.* As we've talked about, surprise is a powerful marketing tactic. It worked well here. Surprise in this case meant presenting the unexpected, especially for a beer commercial.
> ! *The music tie-in* underscored the emotions involved.
> ! *It showed the sensitive side of masculinity.* This doesn't always work to get your messaging talked about, but it supports the tactics of using surprise and the unexpected.

MARKETING TRUTH

Showing a different side to a brand—one that sets you apart from your competitors—gets noticed.

❗ *The message was one of compassion, tugging on the emotions of the viewer.* It was heartwarming, about love and friendship. Who doesn't want to identify with that?

❗ *The ad highlighted the worth of human dignity and life.* Many described the content as "shockingly different."

FOUR SEASONS HEATING AND AIR CONDITIONING: YOUR WIFE IS HOT

Four Seasons Heating and Air Conditioning stuck their neck out when trying to get attention. Sometimes that's what it takes. It's often easier said than done, but the rewards can be huge. Here's their simple ad/billboard headline that got so much attention:

Your Wife Is Hot

What seems like something that's a little on the offensive side turned out to be an idea nothing short of marketing genius. Many customers wrote in about the company's ad campaign. Here's what one said: "Your name and logo had been bombarding me lately. From seeing you listed in the recent *Crain's Chicago Business* list, on the boards at the Blackhawks game, and the fliers that show up in my [local natural gas company] bill. Perhaps the most memorable impression is the 'Your Wife Is Hot' billboard on I-294. I also consulted with a consumer review list and it was pretty obvious I should have Four Seasons come take a look." This reaction was just one of many the company received while running this campaign. The customer ended his testimonial by writing, "I am truly satisfied and confident in selecting Four Seasons. You can be sure that I will be repeating this story to my friends, relatives, and co-workers!"

MARKETING TRUTH

Sometimes what seems a little risqué may not be and may get your prospects' attention so that they engage with your message to see what's behind it.

Getting noticed and getting talked about was no accident. It clearly is part of the company's marketing mission. Will people do business with a company that might be a little on the offensive side with their marketing message? My answer is absolutely yes. Get talked about and get business.

SHARING OSIRIS SHOES CUSTOMER SERVICE WITH FRIENDS

Nothing spreads the word like good customer service, whether you are telling friends and family members or spreading the word via social media and online review sites. The best way to tell you about a superb customer service experience is to let you read the email exchanges between me and the Osiris shoe company regarding a defective pair of shoes.

First email from me to Osiris: "We purchased a pair of Osiris shoes for a Christmas gift this past Christmas. It is my son's fourth or fifth pair, as he is an avid consumer of your product. The latest pair purchased seems defective. Through normal wear and tear the sole of one shoe has detached from the shoe base and totally is torn away from the shoe. I understand wear and tear, but this looks like a defect. We would like to return them for another pair that is not defective. I know you have 30 days as a policy against manufacturing defects but this seems over and above the norm. Can we obtain authorization to return and a credit for new shoes upon your inspection? Thanks for your attention to this matter."

Osiris's response to me: "You are correct, we normally have a 30-day warranty, but we can extend it if it seems that it is a manufacture issue. Can you please email me some pictures of the shoes so I can send them to my manager for review? We will definitely take care of you the best we can."

I sent pictures. This is the company's response after viewing the pictures: "This is definitely a defective product and we need to get you a replacement pair of shoes. Go on our site and visit www.osirisshoes.com. Find your top three choices that we show in your size and we will send a pair for you ASAP. Please provide the styles, the size you want, and the shipping address."

Sizes were sent, along with a shipping address and a closing message from me: "Thanks again and my son wanted me to make sure to thank you as well. We will spread the word about Osiris!"

We actually told many of our experience. Friends and family started sharing with us their purchase of Osiris shoes just because they heard our story of great customer service.

I also told the company how impressed I was with their excellent service and attention to good customers. The company sent out the replacement shoes right away and kept us up-to-date on the status of the order. Osiris turned anxiety into elation. The company understands customer service and what it takes to get others to become raving fans. This is just the type of behavior that generates relationships, customer loyalty, true value, and powerful word-of-mouth.

In all the examples in this chapter, someone told me about them after they first saw it. That's what happens and that's an example of our inherent nature to share and talk about unusual things. Just think, "Give them something to talk about," and your marketing job is on its way to success. Wait; that's the name of the next chapter. Let's take a look.

MARKETING TRUTH

Nothing spreads the word like good customer service.

CHAPTER 18

GIVE THEM SOMETHING TO TALK ABOUT

ALK ABOUT GETTING TALKED ABOUT! THAT'S EXACTLY WHAT University of Louisville women's basketball coach Jeff Walz wanted when he said he would buy beer at the opening season game in 2013. To be specific, Coach Walz agreed to buy 2,500 fans their first beer on $2 beer night at the KFC Yum! Center at the preseason women's game against LSU. The coach called it a sign of gratitude to the Lady Cardinals' loyal fans, along with an encouragement to everyone else to check out his team. The total tab was $5,000 and Coach Walz paid for it with his own money. Aside from being the most popular man on campus that night, the coach got people talking. Getting people to talk draws attention, and in this case it increased attendance. Mission accomplished.

BUYING BEER FOR 2,500 WILL GET YOU TALKED ABOUT

Coach Walz said they just wanted to have a good time at the ballgame and made sure to alert those that would partake in the beer to bring a designated driver—another way to increase the fan base. This was a case where a coach who was passionate about the success of his program wanted to expose as many fans as he could who otherwise probably wouldn't pay attention to the University of Louisville women's basketball team. Get people talking about something new and unique and the masses will flock; at least that was his hope. "It shows his commitment to the program and his desire to grow the program and expose as many fans as possible to their play on the court," said Amy Morgan, Louisville's assistant athletic director.

The University of Louisville gets talked about anyway because of their national men's basketball championship, a women's basketball Final Four appearance, a BCS football win, and a College World Series appearance. The free beer only increases the buzz.

MARKETING TRUTH

Giving people something to talk about will create buzz.

USING BACON TO GET TALKED ABOUT: BACON BUZZ

K-State calls it "bacon basketball." I call it "bacon buzz." Like Coach Walz at the University of Louisville, the Kansas State Wildcats wanted something that would boost attendance at a women's basketball game without distracting attention from any other home sports event. What started out as a joke became a buzz generator. Instead of giving away free pizza, T-shirts, or bobbleheads, the suggestion was made to give away bacon. Free bacon was truly out-of-the-box thinking. Once it was suggested, the free bacon promotion caught on, grew in popularity, and then erupted into a phenomenon.

Here's how it worked: The first 1,000 students with a valid student ID who attended the women's basketball season opener against Tennessee State would each receive five or six slices of bacon. Word of the impending promotion got talked about and spread so quickly by word-of-mouth and social media that Kansas State had to triple its bacon order to its concessionaire, from 100 pounds to 300 pounds. "Bacon basketball" began to buzz and soon attracted national attention. Those talking about it grew exponentially, almost overnight. Is this the next generation of game-day giveaways, as one news source reported? Is the formula for getting talked about combining two of our nation's passions: sports and bacon? One source asked, "We are a fat nation, and we are a nation that loves its sports. Why not combine the two?"

This was a campaign that understood its target market: College kids love free food. There's very little that's more popular than free food to those between the ages of 18 and 22. Participants were encouraged to tweet bacon photos from the evening event. "Bacon buzz" happened. Now it looks like bacon basketball may be here to stay. That's what people are talking about.

You just read lots of good examples, real-life stories and instances where marketing messages were noticed, remembered, and talked about. Now let's wrap it up so you can be on your way to your own marketing successes.

MARKETING TRUTH

Getting people excited about more than one passion will fuel the spreading of a message or campaign.

EPILOGUE

WHETHER IT'S MONTGOMERY WARD SENDING OUT HIS FIRST direct-mail campaign for Sears & Roebuck Company; the advent of Twitter, Facebook, and YouTube; or the sign posted by the florist shop on a corner in your town, marketing has taken wildly different forms and approaches from days of old through to today. New methods, new technology, changing customer habits and demands, new products and services, and a whole new world of communication are only going to give marketers like you more tools and options to use. What will stay the same is that marketers the world over will continue to fight for consumers' attention, mind-share, and their dollar. This, too, will continue, only probably in a more furious way.

In order to thrive and survive, you have to gain consumers' and prospects' attention. You have just learned how to do that and the many methods to use to make it happen. Products, services, companies, and people have to get talked about. Call it marketing buzz, top-of-mind awareness, or viral marketing. You have just learned all about that. At the end of the day, things need to be talked about to reach the critical mass of purchasers that every marketer strives for. That won't ever change. Only the methods will. Technology will. Customers' demands will, too, but the inherent principles of getting noticed, remembered, and talked about won't.

This book has hit on many tactics to help every marketer achieve these goals. Not all of these will work for every situation, but many will. You'll need to prioritize your efforts based on what your target market will respond to and what will fuel your marketing. Some of these methods and tactics are conservative and tried-and-true, while others are extreme, way out-of-the-box, and even abnormal in the course of everyday marketing. Both can work. You have to decide which is best for your situation and market and try them. Experiment, push the envelope, test, and try again, because marketing is made up of many factors working together. To paraphrase an old adage, "Half of your marketing is working; you just don't always know which half it is." That's why testing, experimenting, and becoming a relentless marketer are paramount for any company or organization's success.

I suggest that you pick just a few things in this book that resonate with you, your personality, business, identity, and what you're known for. You can't do everything in this book; no one can. So prioritize and implement. One of the biggest challenges of business today is implementation. Many will read this book and place it on the shelf, forget about it, and start fighting the fire of the day. Those who implement one or two or a few pieces of advice from *Market Like You Mean It*, choosing tips that they are comfortable with, will make more trips to deposit money in the bank. That's the goal. I don't know many people whose business is their hobby. Usually, they have a purpose and many times profit is that purpose. This book will help you achieve that goal of greater profits.

As we wind down, I want to leave you with a few maxims to help you with prioritization. Remember that I suggested that you pick a few things in this book that resonate with you and your style, personality, and identity. These five maxims will help:

1. *Not every marketing initiative to gain attention and create marketing buzz needs to be a stunt or extreme.* Online or offline, people crave information. Sharing is a huge marketing buzzword. Successful businesses and people share ideas, information, and data. Successful businesses and people did this well before the internet; that's how we know it works.

2. *In marketing there is an adage that asks, "Does everyone who can buy from you know about you?"* Chances are, they don't, or no one would be marketing or need to market. Let the world know you exist. That includes publicizing, commenting, tweeting, blogging, and more. If you're going to be relevant you have to be present.

3. *It's still all about the relationship.* You can put all the information you want out there, but unless someone reads it, engages with you, and takes things to the next actionable step, like buying, that information doesn't matter. It takes a relationship to move things along. Spend time helping people to know you, like you, and trust you. That's the ultimate relationship that fuels anything related to marketing.

4. *Marketing is all around you.* Look at all the marketing messages bombarding you every day. Take note of what you think is working. There are stories at work, stunts gaining attention, and buzz happening. Take note.

5. *People buy from people, so you must humanize your brand.* People don't buy from logos. They don't buy from a business name. They buy from people. That means getting attention, developing relationships, fueling the conversation, and giving others a reason to interact, engage, and buy from you, the person. People want to know that you are approachable and a regular person just like them. That's the identity you want to portray. That's what gets noticed and talked about.

It's a given that the marketplace is more crowded than ever before. More marketing messages are coming at you than ever before. The awareness of your products, service, people, and company has never been more important. The one thing that is fought over more than ever is people's attention. Everyone out there wants a piece of it. So get out in front. Own it. Don't lose it.

If you're serious about taking yourself, your company, or your products and services to new levels, let the world know. Get noticed by your key target market and get them talking about you to do your marketing work for you. That's the holy grail of marketing and the pathway to making more deposits in the bank. Happy marketing!

ABOUT THE AUTHOR

A L Lautenslager is a sought-after speaker and the former president and owner of The Ink Well, a commercial printing and mailing company in Wheaton, Illinois. He currently is the principal of Market For Profits, a guerrilla marketing consulting and coaching firm. He is also a multiple "Business of the Year" award winner.

Al is the co-author of *Guerrilla Marketing in 30 Days* (Entrepreneur Press), a bestselling book in the Guerrilla Marketing series, which hit the number-one spot on Amazon in Japan in 2006. He is also the author of *The Ultimate Guide to Direct Marketing* (Entrepreneur Press) and numerous other marketing and business books. He appears regularly on radio and TV as well.

Al has shared the stage with Mayor Rudy Guiliani and has worked with Donald Trump and his TV show, *The Apprentice*. Every year he makes numerous media appearances reviewing Super Bowl TV commercials.

Al has also served as the featured marketing and PR expert for the online version of *Entrepreneur* magazine and is a certified Guerrilla Marketing Coach.

Originally from the Cincinnati, Ohio, area, Al holds an undergraduate degree from Miami University and an MBA in marketing from the University of Dayton. He has extensive experience from engineering to technical to sales and marketing management within the corporate world in addition to his entrepreneurial ventures.

Al is an adjunct instructor within the Wisconsin Technical College system. He also teaches marketing at the MBA level at Concordia University.

The author can be reached via email at al@allautenslager.com.

OTHER BOOKS BY AL LAUTENSLAGER

Guerrilla Marketing in 30 Days (Entrepreneur Press, 2005, Revised 2009 and 2014)

Guerrilla Marketing in 30 Days Workbook (Entrepreneur Press, 2006)

Kick It Up a Notch Marketing: 25 High Impact Marketing Strategies for Real Estate Professionals (Cameo Publications, 2006)

RE: RE-newing, RE-inventing, RE-engineering, RE-positioning, RE-juvenating Your Business and Life (Morgan James Publishing, 2011)

The Ultimate Guide to Direct Marketing (Entrepreneur Press, 2005)

INDEX

A

action, 15, 17. *See also* calls to action

action words, 25–27

acts of kindness, 95–96

AIDA marketing formula, 15–17

"Ain't nobody got time for that" catchphrase, 161–163

Algonquin Hotel, 89–90

animals in advertisements, 36, 93–94, 163

Apple, 22, 115

approachability, 34, 54, 179

asking to get noticed, 68–69

attention, interest, desire, action (AIDA), 15–17

Audi dealer billboard advertisement, 33–34, 134

awareness, 15, 16. *See also* top-of-mind awareness (TOMA)

B

babies in advertisements, 93–94, 163

"bacon basketball" promotion, 174–175

bar signs, 67–68. *See also* humorous content

Basil's Café, 81

Baumgartner, Felix, 74–76

Beats by Dr. Dre, 148–149

benefits vs. features, 114, 115, 120, 124, 126–127

Beyoncé, 83–84, 162

Bic Razor billboard advertisement, 33

Bieber, Justin, 145–148

Big Gas Savings commercial, 63

billboard marketing, 32–34, 77–78, 134, 169

Blendtec videos, 118–119

BMW dealer billboard
 advertisement, 33–34, 134–135
bold content, 68–69, 77–78, 84. *See
 also* content
Bondi Beach Bookshelf, 139–140
Brand, Nicholas, 73
brand bites. *See* taglines
brand equity, 9
brand voice, 22
brands, humanizing, 119–120, 179
Branson, Richard, 133–134, 135
British Airways, 133–134
buzz marketing, 21–23. *See also*
 marketing buzz

C
"Call Me Maybe" (song), 131–132
calls to action, 17, 113–115, 138–139
Candid Camera (TV show), 42
Caples, John, 29
catchphrases, 161–163
challenge headlines, 30–31. *See also*
 headlines
church signs, 65–66. *See also*
 humorous content
Clinton, Hillary, 38, 155
cocktails, 89–91
Coconut Greetings, 92
coffee shop stunt, 41, 78–80. *See also*
 promotional stunts
community participation, 155–157,
 159–160. *See also* social media
 marketing
compelling content, 11, 23–24,
 28–30, 32–33. *See also* content
competition, 133–135. *See also*
 differentiation
competitive advantage, 114, 115, 127.
 See also differentiation
comps, 95–96

consistency, 53, 100, 106, 113, 114,
 151
content. *See also* messaging
 billboard, 32–34, 77–78, 134, 169
 bold, 68–69, 77–78, 84
 compelling, 11, 23–24, 28–30,
  32–33
 controversial, 63, 84–87, 124, 164
 dramatic, 23–24, 53–54
 email subject line, 28, 99, 100, 101
 engaging, 12–13, 39–41, 59–61,
  76–77, 102, 123–127, 132
 exciting, 21–23, 175
 headline, 4, 5–6, 27–32, 33–34,
  138, 169
 how-to, 108–109
 humorous, 59–68, 106
 interesting, 10, 12, 13, 19–21,
  27–33, 102–106, 138
 marketing hook, 6–7, 102–103,
  139
 negative, 38–39, 119, 121, 138
 packaging of, 13
 power words in, 25–27
 provocative, 5–6, 16, 24, 138
 repurposing, 5, 10–11
 sign, 65–68
 solution-oriented, 5, 12
 thought-provoking, 51, 65, 138
 topic ideas for, 11–12
 unconventional. *See* unconventional messaging
content marketing, 10–13, 41, 101,
 103, 107–109, 125, 150–152. *See
 also* messaging
controversial content, 63, 84–87,
 124, 164. *See also* content;
 unconventional messaging
copywriting, 29. *See also* content;
 messaging

credibility, 45, 150. *See also* trust
customer service, 140, 170–171
cuteness factor, 36, 93–95, 163

D
Deen, Paula, 57–58
desire, 15, 16–17, 39, 40, 117. *See also* emotional connections
dialog, 107
differentiation, 13–15, 34–35, 73–74, 97–98, 102. *See also* competition; competitive advantage; standing out
direct mail, 43, 45, 91–93, 138
Dos Equis advertising campaign, 19–20
dramatic content, 23–24, 53–54. *See also* content

E
earworms, 131–132
easel signs, 67. *See also* humorous content
electronic billboards, 33. *See also* billboard marketing
email marketing, 28, 99–101
emotional connections
  desire and, 15, 16–17, 39, 40, 117
  in email marketing, 101
  with guerrilla marketing tactics, 139
  in Guinness commercial, 167–169
  in headlines, 31–32
  in messaging, 4
  for motivating prospects, 23
  negative campaign ads, 39
  purchase decisions and, 9
  social transmission and, 117–120
  stories and, 47–58, 70
  with surprise marketing, 81
  in taglines, 127

top-of-mind awareness (TOMA) and, 51–52
  triggers of, 39–41
  in videos, 106
emotional hooks, 40–41
emotion-based headlines, 31–32. *See also* headlines
engagement, 12–13, 39–41, 59–61, 76–77, 102, 123–127, 132. *See also* interest; interesting content
excitement, 21–23, 175
expert positioning, 14, 22, 97–98, 108–109
extreme headlines, 31, 33. *See also* headlines
extreme marketing, 6, 138. *See also* unconventional messaging
extreme skydiving stunt, 74–77. *See also* promotional stunts

F
fear, 39–40. *See also* emotional connections
flash mobs, 71–73. *See also* unconventional messaging
Fogle, Jared, 53–56
Ford Motor Company billboard advertisement, 34
Four Seasons Heating and Air Conditioning advertising, 169–170
free bacon promotion, 174–175
free beer promotion, 173–174
free reports, 6, 102–103, 164
frequency, 44–45, 100, 106. *See also* repetition

G
General Electric, 115
Ginsberg, Scott, 34–35
GoDaddy.com commercials, 37, 84–86

Goodyear blimp, 81–82
graphics, 4, 6, 13, 32–33, 138
guerrilla marketing, 135, 137–140
Guinness commercial, 167–169

H
H&M fashion retailer Super Bowl
    commercial, 35–36
Halfway, Oregon, 69–70
halo effect, 9
hashtags, 104, 164
headlines, 4, 5–6, 27–32, 33–34, 138,
    169. *See also* content; subject lines
    in emails
Hill, Faith, 64
Holiday Inn Express advertisement,
    7, 139
how-to content, 108–109. *See also*
    content
how-to headlines, 30. *See also*
    headlines
humanizing brands, 119–120, 179
humorous content, 59–68, 106. *See*
    also content; unconventional
    messaging

I
IKEA Bondi Beach Bookshelf,
    139–140
impact words, 25–27. *See also*
    content
implementation strategies, 177–180
Improv Everywhere, 71
inbound marketing, 107
influence marketing, 10, 143–144,
    152–153. *See also* social media
    marketing
information, offering, 6, 12, 102–103,
    164
interest, 5–7, 15–16, 129. *See also*
    engagement
interesting content, 10, 12, 13,
19–21, 27–33, 102–106, 138. *See*
    also content; engagement

J
Jepsen, Carly Rae, 131–132
Jetsetter, 13
Jobs, Steve, 48
Joel, Billy, 68–69
junk mail, 5, 100

K
Kmart advertising, 62–63

L
lead generation, 107
Levinson, Jay Conrad, 44
Lewis, E. St. Elmo, 15
likability, 14–15, 94
loyalty, 13, 77, 94–95, 148, 150–151,
    171. *See also* trust
lumpy mail, 91–93, 138
luxury, 33–34, 89–91, 134

M
mailing pieces, 7, 43, 91–93, 138
market knowledge, 14
marketing buzz. *See also* influence
    marketing; viral marketing; word-
    or-mouth marketing
    Bests by Dr. Dre, 148–149
    defined, 144
    exciting content for, 21–23, 175
    Four Seasons Heating and Air
        Conditioning advertising,
        169–170
    free bacon promotion, 174–175
    free beer promotion, 173–174
    Guinness commercial, 167–169
    humorous content for, 59–68, 106
    influence marketing for, 10, 143–
        144, 152–153
    Justin Bieber success story,
        145–148

Osiris Shoes customer service,
170–171
prioritization maxims about,
179
promotional stunts for, 41–43,
74–80, 86–87
relevance in, 101, 125, 150–152
social media for, 8, 10, 109, 146–
148, 155–157
stories and, 51
top-of-mind awareness (TOMA)
and, 42–44, 50–53, 60, 62,
125, 132, 134, 155–157
unconventional tactics for. *See*
unconventional messaging
marketing hooks, 6–7, 102–103,
139
marketing messages. *See* messaging
marquee signs, 67. *See also*
humorous content
memory, 126, 129–132
Men in Kilts, 73–74
messaging. *See also* content; content
marketing
best practices in, 66
in billboard marketing, 77–78
brand voice in, 22
clear, 6, 113, 114
compelling, 11, 23–24, 28–30,
32–33
competition and, 133–135
consistent, 53, 100, 106, 113, 114,
151
engaging, 12–13, 39–41, 59–61,
76–77, 102, 123–127, 132
exciting, 21–23, 175
frequency of, 44–45, 100, 106
goal of, 25
headlines in, 4, 5–6, 27–32,
33–34, 138, 169
humorous, 59–68, 106

interesting, 10, 12, 13, 19–21,
27–33, 102–106, 138
personalizing, 24
in political ads, 38–39
relevant, 101, 125, 150–152
repetition in, 36, 43–45, 60, 114
standing out in, 3–7, 11–15,
23–24, 32–33, 89–90, 105,
107–109, 139
stickiness in, 131–132
stories as, 47–58
in Super Bowl commercials,
35–38
unconventional. *See* unconventional messaging
viral, 159–165. *See also* viral marketing
wording in, 25–27
Mini Cooper Super Bowl
commercial, 64
mnemonic devices, 130
motivating to take action, 15, 17,
21–23, 39–40, 113–115, 118–119,
151

N
nametags, 34–35
Nantucket Nectars, 49–50
negative content, 38–39, 119, 121,
138. *See also* content
Nike, 49

O
O'Donovan's Irish Pub, 77–78
online communities, 155–157. *See
also* social media marketing;
social sharing
online marketing, 97–109. *See also*
influence marketing; social media
marketing
Osiris Shoes customer service,
170–171

outbound marketing, 107
outrageous tactics, 38, 41–43,
  69–71. *See also* unconventional
  messaging

P
pain points, 12
Parsons, Bob, 37
Patrick, Danica, 37
Perfect Match commercial, 85–86
personalizing messaging, 24
political ads, 38–39
Pollack, Michael, 68–69
popularity, 120–121
positioning, 13–14, 22, 97–98,
  108–109, 114, 125, 164. *See also*
  taglines
power words, 25–27
prankvertising, 41–43. *See
  also* promotional stunts;
  unconventional messaging
Procter & Gamble "Thank You,
  Mom" campaign, 114–115
promotional stunts, 41–43, 71–80,
  86–87. *See also* unconventional
  messaging
provocative content, 5–6, 16, 24, 138.
  See also content; unconventional
  messaging
psychology of marketing, 8–10
psychology of social transmission,
  117–121
puppies in advertisements, 93–94
purchase decisions, 8–10, 36

R
Ray, Rachael, 56–58
Red Bull Stratos stunt, 74–77. *See
  also* promotional stunts
Red Robin restaurant, 95–96
relationship building, 8–9, 12–13, 45,
  100–101, 103–105, 144, 151, 179

relationship marketing, 14–15
relevance, 101, 125, 150–152
remarkability, 34–35
repetition, 36, 43–45, 60, 114. *See
  also* frequency
reports online, 6, 102–103, 164
repurposing content, 5, 10–11. *See
  also* content

S
Samsung campaign, 115
search engine optimization (SEO), 109
search engine results, 28
sharing, 52–53, 117–121, 152–153,
  179. *See also* viral marketing
shock and surprise, 41–43,
  72, 77–87, 106. *See also*
  unconventional messaging
showerhead advertisement, 7, 139
signs, 65–68. *See also* humorous
  content
slogans, 74, 125–127, 129, 131
'sNice Café stunt, 41, 78–80. *See also*
  promotional stunts
social loyalty, 94–95. *See also* loyalty;
  trust
social media marketing, 8, 10, 109,
  146–148, 155–157. *See also*
  influence marketing
social psychology, 117–121
social sharing, 52–53, 117–121, 152–
  153, 179. *See also* viral marketing
solution-oriented content, 5, 12. *See
  also* content
Southwest Airlines, 60–61
spam, 99, 100
standing out, 3–7, 11–15, 23–24,
  32–33, 89–90, 105, 107–109,
  139. *See also* differentiation;
  unconventional messaging
Starbucks, 91, 148

stories, 47–58, 70

story headlines, 30. *See also* headlines

stuck song syndrome, 131–132

stunts, 41–43, 71–80, 86–87. *See also* unconventional messaging

subject lines in emails, 28, 99, 100, 101. *See also* headlines

Subway sandwich chain, 53–56

Successful Advertising (Smith), 43–44

Super Bowl commercials, 35–38, 60, 62, 64, 85

surprise marketing, 41–43, 72, 77–84. *See also* unconventional messaging

Sweet Brown, 161–163

T

Taco Bell controversy, 86–87. *See also* controversial content; promotional stunts

taglines, 74, 125–127, 129, 131. *See also* positioning

targeted headlines, 31. *See also* headlines

targeted marketing, 5, 28–29, 73–74, 106, 114, 151

tastemakers, 159

Teleflora Super Bowl commercial, 64

"Thank You, Mom" campaign, 114–115

Thinkmodo agency, 43

thought leadership, 51, 72, 108, 109

thought-provoking content, 51, 65, 138. *See also* content

three-dimensional mail, 91–93, 138

titles, 5–6

top-of-mind awareness (TOMA), 42–44, 50–53, 60, 62, 125, 132, 134, 155–157. *See also* marketing buzz

touch points, 43–44, 67, 72, 127, 139

trust, 8–9, 12, 14–15, 40, 98–99, 108, 144, 150–152. *See also* loyalty

Truth or Consequences, New Mexico, 70

U

unconventional messaging. *See also* humorous content; messaging; standing out

in Audi/BMW billboard war, 33–34, 134–135

in church signs, 65–66

controversial content, 63, 84–87, 124, 164

extreme marketing, 6, 38

flash mobs and, 71–73

in IKEA Bondi Beach Bookshelf marketing, 139–140

in Men in Kilts marketing, 73–74

outrageous tactics, 38, 41–43, 69–71

pranks and stunts, 41–43, 71–80, 86–87

provocative content, 5–6, 16, 24, 138

psychological advantage of, 10

shock and surprise, 41–43, 72, 77–87, 106

three-dimensional mail, 91–93, 138

unique selling propositions, 13

V

veterinary signs, 67. *See also* humorous content

videos, 62–63, 64, 79, 106, 118–120, 139, 146–147, 159–165

viral marketing

buzz marketing and, 21–23

emotions and, 40

flash mobs and, 71–73
Guinness commercial, 167–169
humor in, 62, 64, 74
pranks and stunts for, 41–43,
    71–80, 86–87. *See also*
    unconventional messaging
social sharing and, 52–53, 117–
    121, 152–153, 179
surprise tactics and, 84
videos and, 62–63, 64, 79, 106,
    118–120, 139, 146–147,
    159–165
Virgin Airlines, 133–134
visualization, 130

W
WestJet's Christmas Miracle video,
    160–161
Wilkins, Kimberly, 161–163
word-of-mouth marketing, 10, 74,
    81, 143–149, 152–153, 171, 175.
    See also marketing buzz
WOW factor, 89–96

Y
"you", using in marketing messages,
    27